What's Wrong with the European Union
and How to Fix It

What's Wrong with the European Union and How to Fix It

SIMON HIX

polity

First published in 2008 by Polity Press

Polity Press
65 Bridge Street
Cambridge CB2 1UR, UK.

Polity Press
350 Main Street
Malden, MA 02148, USA

ISBN-13: 978-07456-4204-8
ISBN-13: 978-07456-4205-5 (pb)

A catalogue record for this book is available from the British Library.

Typeset in 10.25 on 13 pt FF Scala
by Servis Filmsetting Ltd, Manchester
Printed and bound in Great Britain by MPG Books Ltd, Bodmin, Cornwall

The publisher has used its best endeavours to ensure that the URLs for
external websites referred to in this book are correct and active at the time of
going to press. However, the publisher has no responsibility for the websites
and can make no guarantee that a site will remain live or that the content is or
will remain appropriate.

Every effort has been made to trace all copyright holders, but if any have been
inadvertently overlooked the publishers will be pleased to include any
necessary credits in any subsequent reprint or edition.

For further information on Polity, visit our website: www.polity.co.uk

Contents

Figures

Tables

Boxes

Preface

Although I wrote this book in the first few months of 2007 it is the product of several years of research, thinking and teaching about the European Union (EU). I have always been interested in how political science can use theoretical insights and empirical analysis to contribute to public policy and political reform. I was lucky enough to have the opportunity to engage directly with policy-makers on the issue of reform of the EU when I chaired a working group on 'Democracy in the EU' for the British Cabinet Office during the Convention on the Future of Europe. This was one of several working groups convened by the British government to discuss the British position in the EU constitutional reform process.

Since then, I have developed my ideas about the problems facing the EU and what could be done to address them in a series of lectures and seminars. These included presentations at the Institut d'études politiques (Sciences-Po) in Paris, Harvard University, a British Council–Foreign Policy Centre conference in Taormina in Sicily, the University of Essex, the College of Europe at Natolin in Poland, Yonsei University in Seoul, the University of Tokyo, the European Policy Centre in Brussels, the University of Copenhagen, the University of California in Berkeley, the British–Dutch government conference on subsidiarity in the Hague, Princeton University, the Free University in Brussels, the European Central Bank in Frankfurt, the University of Zurich, Charles University in Prague, and the conference of the presidents of the EU parliaments on the 50th

anniversary of the Treaty of Rome, at the European University
Institute in Florence in March 2007. I would like to thank all
those who participated in these seminars and commented on
my ideas, in particular Stefano Bartolini, Lars-Erik Cederman,
Barry Eichengreen, Baron Frankel, Mark Franklin, Peter Hall,
Stefan Huemer, Michiel van Hulten, Simon Hug, Hae-Won
Jun, Jo Leinen, Mark Leonard, Johannes Lindner, Andrew
Moravcsik, John Palmer, Michael Shackleton and Alexander
Trechsel.

I also developed my ideas on the democratic accountability
of the EU and the design and operation of the EU institutions
in several articles, books and policy papers. Some of the ideas
in this book draw on these previous publications, some of
which were co-authored. I am very much indebted to my co-
authors of this previous work: Abdul Noury, Gérard Roland,
Andreas Føllesdal and Michael Marsh.

I would also like to thank Giacomo Benedetto, Ben Crum,
David Farrell, Matthew Gabel, David Held and Tom Hitchings
for offering very helpful comments on the draft manuscript.
Finally, I would like to thank my wife, Beth, and my children,
Ben and Ruth, for enduring my absences while travelling to
present and develop the ideas in this book.

Simon Hix
London
November, 2007

Abbreviations

ALDE   Alliance of Liberals and Democrats for Europe,
            the centrist/liberal group in the European
            Parliament since June 2004
CFSP   Common Foreign and Security Policy
EDD   Group of European Democracies and
            Diversities, the anti-European group in the
            European Parliament until June 2004
ELDR   European Liberal, Democrat and Reform Party,
            the centrist/liberal transnational party, and a
            group in the European Parliament until June
            2004
EMU   Economic and monetary union
EPP(-ED)   European People's Party(-European Democrats),
            the centre-right group in the European Parliament
EU15   The EU of fifteen member states before enlarge-
            ment in May 2004
EU25   The EU of twenty-five member states between
            the enlargement in May 2004 and the enlarge-
            ment in January 2007
EU27   The EU of twenty-seven member states after the
            enlargement in January 2007
EUL/NGL   European United Left/Nordic Green Left, the
            radical left group in the European Parliament
G/EFA   Greens/European Free Alliance, the coalition
            of greens and regionalists in the European
            Parliament

IND/DEM	Independence/Democracy, the anti-European group in the European Parliament from June 2004
MEPs	Members of the European Parliament
NA	non-attached Members of the European Parliament
PES	Party of European Socialists, the centre-left transnational party and group in the European Parliament
QMV	qualified-majority voting, the system of weighted voting in the EU Council
SQ	status quo, the current (fallback) policy
UEN	Union for a Europe of Nations, the conservative/nationalist group in the European Parliament

CHAPTER ONE

Introduction

For decades Europe's leaders have pretended that there is no politics in Brussels. The European Union works through politically neutral institutions and happy consensus, so they claim, epitomised by the 'family photo' of smiling heads of government at each quarterly European Council meeting. This is a charade. Beneath the surface neutrality and consensus are ferocious political battles. These battles used to be about how far and how fast European integration should proceed. These days, however, they are about how far and how fast European economic and social policies should be reformed.

On one side of the new debate are the reformers, who want economic and social change in Europe. The unofficial leader of this group is Commission President José Manuel Barroso, supported by most of his fellow commissioners, most centre-right and 'modern' social democrat governments, particularly from the new member states, and the centre-right and liberal Members of the European Parliament (MEPs). On the other side are the supporters of the traditional European social model. This group is most vocally represented by the French left, and includes several left-wing governments, a few 'traditional' socialist Commissioners, many of the socialist, green and radical left MEPs, and assorted organised labour groups and NGOs throughout the continent.

This, I believe, is exactly what Europe needs. For too long the EU has been isolated from real political debate. Delegating powers to politically independent institutions, and making decisions largely by consensus, was a good idea during the construction of the basic economic and political architecture of the EU, to ensure a neutral design of our continental-scale polity. However, now that this architecture is in place, the EU faces three new challenges, each of which requires more open political debate at the European level.

The first challenge is how to overcome 'policy gridlock'. The EU needs to undertake reforms to make the European economy generate more jobs and increase growth while protecting the European way of life, for example through the reform of labour markets, the service sector, the energy sector and the welfare state. These are tough policy decisions, which the EU has thus far been unable to take. These decisions are also fundamentally 'political', since any changes to existing policies will produce winners and losers, at least in the short term, and these winners and losers will take different sides in the debate. Difficult policy decisions also require leadership, as reforms cannot be undertaken without a coalition in support of them within and across the EU institutions.

The second challenge is the low and declining level of popular legitimacy of the EU. Only about 50 per cent of EU citizens currently think that their county's membership of the EU is 'a good thing'. The long-term viability of the EU is questionable unless the downward trend in support for the project can be reversed in the next decade. Without a mandate for policy change, economic reform directed from Brussels is likely to reduce rather than increase public support for the EU. The winners from reforms may become more enthusiastic about the EU, but the losers will become even more opposed.

The third challenge is how to make the EU more democratically accountable. The EU is certainly democratic in procedural terms, in that we elect our governments and MEPs, who together appoint the Commission and make policy in our name in Brussels. In substantive terms, however, the EU is closer to a form of enlightened despotism than a genuine democracy. The representative structures and the checks-and-balances of decision-making ensure that EU policies are relatively centrist, and hence close to the views of most European citizens. However, without a genuine debate about and competition over the exercise of political authority at the European level, most people do not know what their views are about major policy issues on the EU agenda and have no way of influencing the direction of the EU policy agenda even if they did.

The choice for our political leaders is not between focusing on policy reform or focusing on improving the legitimacy and accountability of the EU. In reality, policy reform will inevitably lead to political conflicts, and the outcomes of these conflicts will not be accepted as legitimate by those on the losing side unless there has been an open and democratic debate about the reform options which produces a mandate for policy change.

More politics in the EU should not be feared. Rather, it should be embraced. Competition for public office and over the policy agenda forces elites to engage in policy innovation. Politics encourages 'joined up thinking' across issues, where the policies in one area (such as labour market liberalisation) have to be matched with policies in other areas (such as higher spending on education and training). Politics allows coalitions to be built across institutions, and so would enable the EU to overcome the checks-and-balances in the system. Politics would provide incentives for TV and newspaper editors to be interested in the 'Brussels soap opera' for the first time. Above all, more open EU politics would encourage citizens to understand the policy options, to identify which leaders take what positions on the key issues, to take sides in European-level policy debates, and ultimately to accept being on the losing side in the short term in the expectation of being on the winning side in the near future.

So, what the EU needs, I contend, is 'limited democratic politics'. I use the word 'limited' here to mean two things: first, limited rather than full democratic politics, as I think the public is not ready for full-blown European-wide direct democracy; and, second, limited meaning heavily constrained by the existing checks-and-balances of the EU system. The EU never will be, and never should be, like the Westminster model of government, where a narrow political majority can dictate policy outcomes. But the EU should become more like the German or Scandinavian models, where a broad coalition is built in support of policy changes via open and vigorous political debate.

There are two prerequisites for limited democratic politics: (1) an *institutional* design that allows for a contest for leadership and control of the policy agenda, at least for a limited period; and (2) a pattern of elite *behaviour* where contestation is accepted and where losers in decisions are willing to accept the legitimacy of the winners. It might come as a surprise to some people that the EU actually possesses both these elements already.

On the institutional side, treaty reforms since the mid 1980s have transformed the EU into a considerably more majoritarian system. Qualified-majority voting (QMV) in the Council now covers all the main areas relating to the creation and reform of the internal market. The European Parliament has co-equal power with the Council under the co-decision procedure in almost all areas of social and economic regulation. Finally, the introduction of QMV in the European Council for choosing the Commission president and the Commission as a whole will gradually transform the way the Commission is 'elected'. This may seem a relatively innocuous change. However, the new rules for electing the Commission now mean that the same coalition of governments in the Council and political parties in the European Parliament can elect 'their' agenda-setter and then pass his or her legislative proposals.

On the elite behaviour side, ideological (left–right) battles are now a strong feature in all three EU institutions. The left–right is the main dimension of conflict in the European Parliament; voting in the European Parliament is increasingly along party lines and decreasingly along national lines, and the transnational parties in the European Parliament are now more cohesive than the Democrats and Republicans in the US Congress. The Council has begun to show something similar: with more open contestation and splits along left–right lines. And, the relations between the Commission and the other two EU institutions are increasingly partisan. Whereas the Santer Commission was a grand coalition, the Prodi Commission had a slight centre-left majority, and the Barroso Commission is dominated by centre-right politicians. One of the positive features of conflicts based on left–right splits rather than national divisions is that a winning coalition at the European level is likely to be supported by a section of the elite in every member state.

In fact, since January 2005 the EU has had 'unified centre-right government', with the same coalition of conservatives, liberals and Christian democrats dominating the Commission, the Council and the European Parliament. Not surprisingly, in the Spring of 2005, in the French and Dutch referendums on the EU Constitution, the left mobilised against the neoliberal policies of this EU centre-right coalition.

But, referendums are a crude and ineffectual mechanism for expressing citizens' preferences on EU policy issues. What is missing is a more open debate about the emerging politics inside the Brussels beltway and clearer connections between this politics and citizens' views. Citizens recognise the importance of the EU but do not engage with EU politics. National elections are, understandably, fought on national rather than European issues. Ironically, European Parliament elections also have very little to do with Europe. These elections are not about rival candidates for the Commission President, or about which party should be the largest group in the European Parliament, or even about whether a particular MEP has done a good or bad job. Instead, citizens, the media and national parties treat European Parliament elections as just another set of domestic elections, on the performance and policies of national parties and leaders.

Europe is not ready for full-blown European-wide democracy, as the failure of European Parliament elections to promote European-wide politics has demonstrated. However, by moderately increasing the incentives for elites to compete more openly in Brussels, citizens will begin to understand and engage with EU politics, and may gradually demand to be involved more directly. In procedural terms, further treaty reforms, as in the revised version of the failed Constitution that the EU heads of government agreed in October 2007, will not by themselves change the way politics in the EU works. The institutions already exist for limited democratic politics in the EU. And, even if a new set of treaty reforms are eventually implemented, the EU will still suffer from policy gridlock, a lack of popular legitimacy and a democratic deficit. What is needed is for the political elites to change the way they operate within the institutional rules of the EU.

For example, if a majority coalition in the European Parliament was able to dominate policy-making inside the chamber, there would be more at stake in European Parliament elections. This would encourage national parties and European parties to coordinate their campaigns, as who wins the elections would matter for the first time. The Council, meanwhile, should operate more like a normal legislature, with fully-open legislative deliberations and the publication of amendments to bills and the positions taken by the governments on each issue. And, there should be a more open battle for the Commission President, with rival candidates before European Parliament elections, programmes from each candidate, public debates between the candidates, and declarations of support for each candidate by prime ministers, opposition parties and the European Parliament parties.

What I do in this book is develop this argument. Part I analyses the three main challenges facing the EU: of policy gridlock, a lack of popular legitimacy and the democratic deficit. Part II then makes the case for the gradual development of limited democratic politics in the EU, explains how this has already begun to emerge inside and between the institutions in Brussels, and includes a set of concrete proposals for how more open political contestation in the EU can be encouraged without treaty reform. First, however, I shall make the case for the EU, as for some readers this may not be self-evident.

CHAPTER TWO

Why the European Union is more necessary than ever

How large does an economy need to be to generate enough wealth for its citizens? How small does a polity need to be for the government to be stable and accountable? A recurrent problem since the emergence of industrial society and the spread of democratic government is that the answers to these questions have tended to point in opposite directions.[1]

On the economic side, larger and more diverse economies are generally better than smaller ones. A large economic area allows for greater geographic and human diversity, which enables greater specialisation and economies of scale, which in turn promotes a broader range of goods and services, lower per capita costs of public goods, higher productivity rates, and higher employment, growth and wealth.[2] Sure, small societies, such as Switzerland and Norway, and even micro-states, such as Singapore and Hong Kong, have had highly successful economies. However, they have been successful only because they have been open to and integrated with the rest of the world and have been willing to accept the loss of sovereignty that is an inevitable cost of this openness. Larger societies, and the United States is the epitome of course, have not had to be so economically integrated with the outside world, have not had to specialise on a few key products and services, and have been less affected by the ups and downs of the global economy. In contrast, small states have only been able to prosper in an open global trading system by specialising in a few key goods and by adapting their domestic policies to fit standards set by larger economies.[3] Economic logic suggests, then, that bigger is generally better than smaller, unless a society is able to be internationally competitive in a global free-trading system and is willing to give up autonomy over most macro- and micro-economic policy decisions.

On the political side, in contrast, smaller and more homogeneous societies tend to be more governable than larger and more heterogeneous societies. Smaller societies allow for greater direct participation in government and ensure that political elites are less distant from the people. Furthermore, ethnically, religiously, linguistically and/or culturally homogeneous societies tend to have more harmonious political debates and more shared opinions – what political scientists call 'preferences' – across a range of political issues.[4] Following this logic, Gabriel Almond, Seymour Martin Lipset and others famously argued in the 1950s and 1960s that democracy can only work well either in homogeneous societies or in societies where there are 'cross-cutting cleavages'; meaning that ethnic, religious, economic and cultural divisions overlap to such an extent that all social groups are minorities.[5] Where a society is deeply split between several ethnic or cultural groups, either democratic government is impossible or government by the majority must be heavily constrained by power-sharing between the groups' elites, through grand coalitions.[6] To reiterate the point: contrast successful and stable democratic government in places such as Sweden and the United States, as examples of homogeneous and cross-cutting cleavages, respectively, with unstable or undemocratic government in large diverse and ethnically dived societies such as China, Russia and much of Africa. Some smaller nations, such as Belgium and Switzerland, have been able to resolve cultural conflicts precisely because they are small, which allows for cooperative behaviour between the elites from the rival groups. In general, though, political logic suggests that democratic government works best in smaller and more homogeneous polities.

This helps explain why the United States has been so successful. The United States has a continental-scale economy with a high level of geographic diversity. With such a large domestic economy, only about 20 per cent of the Gross Domestic Product (GDP) of the United States is traded in the global economy. As the world's largest market, rather than having to follow standards and policies set by other economies, the US (until the emergence of the EU) was the international policy leader – forcing other societies to adapt to the regulatory standards and policy choices of the US political and economic decision-makers. Also, US society is highly pluralist, but no single cultural group is dominant, the cultural, religious and socio-economic cleavages are cross-cutting rather than reinforcing, and the polity operates through a common language. As a result, the US has an ideal political-economic model.

No other part of the world has been as fortunate as the US, able to combine an economy which is sufficiently large with a democratically accountable and stable political system on a continental scale. In China and the Soviet Union, the tension between the economic logic of a large state and the political logic of a small and homogenous state was solved by the creation of large economies with undemocratic governments. When democracy came in 1989, the Soviet Union broke up and Russia has gradually slid back towards authoritarian government, in part in reaction to further secessionist demands. One fear of the Beijing elite is that democratic reforms might have a similar effect in China, by unleashing secessionist demands in Tibet, Outer Mongolia and parts of Western China.

Until the last half-century, Western Europe solved the political-economy dilemma in the opposite way to Russia and China: with the creation of small sovereign states. Most of these states were not economically viable on their own, particularly with the development of industrial society and the resultant demands for raw materials and greater labour specialisation. Britain and France responded to these economic pressures with overseas expansion, using colonial empires to fuel their domestic economies. Germany, meanwhile, sought expansion within Europe, by first creating a larger unified national economy and then seeking to capture the territories of neighbouring countries. The result of the competition between the European states was two bloody European civil wars, which dragged other parts of the world into the European power struggle.

Put in this historical and global perspective, the European Union is an extraordinary achievement, in that it is the first attempt outside the United States to create a sustainable *and* accountable polity on a continental scale and hence aim to resolve the opposing economic and political logics. On the economic side, the EU has a continental-scale market, with huge diversity in terms of geography and human expertise. Like the US, only about 20 per cent of the collective GDP of the EU is traded with the rest of the world while the remaining 80 per cent is produced and consumed domestically. On the political side, the EU is a multilevel system of government, which allows European citizens to make decisions about the regulation of the continent-wide market at the European level while maintaining power over taxation and spending at the national level. Further, whereas the US was to some extent a result of good fortune (and some rather clever founding fathers!), the EU is the product of a series of voluntary choices by Europe's leaders and citizens.

As a result of this new political and economic architecture in Europe, the rest of the world is no longer plagued by Europe's failure to find an effective solution to its internal problems. The EU has also been a driving force of global economic and political integration and has become a model for other regions in the world which are still struggling to find an effective balance between economics and politics, such as Latin America, East Asia and West Africa. The EU model is far from perfect, particularly on the political side, but it is a considerable improvement on the alternatives: a continental-scale economy governed by an authoritarian regime, or a patchwork of small states that either are not economically viable or are economically integrated into a broader regional or global economic system but are then not fully sovereign.

The rest of this chapter explains in more detail how the EU solves the tension between economics and politics. I first look at the economics before turning to the politics.

Economics: a continental-scale market in a global economy

The reforms of the EU treaties in the 1980s and 1990s established a new economic and political architecture for the EU: a 'constitution' in all but name. Under the new design, the European level is exclusively responsible for the creation and regulation of the world's largest single market: with over 480 million citizens and almost 30 per cent of total world GDP. The EU's 'internal market' was launched on 1 January 1993, although the completion of this market is an on-going project since numerous technical and non-tariff barriers still limit the genuinely free movement of goods, services, capital and labour between the twenty-seven EU member states (particularly in the areas of services and labour).

To create a level playing field for economic competition and to correct for potential 'market failures' in a European-wide market – such as unfair competition, environmental pollution and the exploitation of workers – the EU has common policies in a range of areas, including competition policy, product standards, environmental standards and basic labour market rules.

While the EU level is responsible for creating the continent-wide market and agreeing on these market-correcting regulations, almost all other areas of public policy remain at the national level in Europe. The EU has very little influence over the major areas of taxation and public spending, such as education, healthcare, transport, housing, welfare provision and pensions. The EU also has very little direct power over justice and interior policies, such as immigration, policing and criminal justice. Nevertheless, keeping these policies at the national level in a single market can lead to what are called 'negative externalities': where a change of policy in one state can have a detrimental effect on the policies of the other EU states. As a result, the national governments recognised that they need to coordinate some of their national policies, such as common macro-economic policy goals and common rules on asylum and economic rights of third-country nationals.

In other words, the basic EU economic policy architecture has been carefully designed to promote market integration in Europe, which necessarily entails some common social and economic rules, while maintaining separate national choices on most of the main areas of economic and security policy.

This model greatly benefits the European economy because of the very high level of economic integration between the EU member states. Figure 2.1 shows the levels of market integration and trade integration in the EU25 states in 2005. All the EU member states trade more with the other members of the EU than with the rest of the world. On average, almost 70 per cent of the total trade of an EU state is with another EU state. Even for the United Kingdom, about 56 per cent of British trade in 2005 was with the other 24 EU states while only 44 per cent was with the more than 100 other countries in the world put together.

Trade with the other EU states also constitutes a huge proportion of the GDP of every member of the EU. For example,

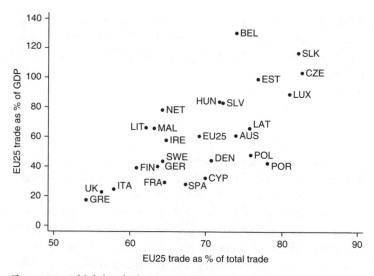

Figure 2.1 A high level of economic integration in Europe

Note: The X-axis is the value of trade with the rest of the EU (imports plus exports) as a percentage of a member state's GDP in 2005. The Y-axis is the percentage of trade with the rest of the EU as a percentage of the total external trade of a member state in 2005.

Source: Eurostat.

Key:						
AUS	Austria	GER	Germany	NET	Netherlands
BEL	Belgium	GRE	Greece	POL	Poland
CYP	Cyprus	HUN	Hungary	POR	Portugal
CZE	Czech Republic	IRE	Ireland	SLK	Slovakia
DEN	Denmark	ITA	Italy	SLN	Slovenia
EU25	EU25 average	LAT	Latvia	SPA	Spain
EST	Estonia	LIT	Lithuania	SWE	Sweden
FIN	Finland	LUX	Luxembourg	UK	United Kingdom
FRA	France	MAL	Malta		

for the United Kingdom, which is the fifth largest economy in the world and has a comparatively high level of trade with other parts of the world, almost 30 per cent of British GDP is traded with the rest of the EU. Hence, the removal of barriers to trade within the EU, and other EU policies that promote economic integration in the European internal market, contribute significantly to all the EU member states, with no exception.

In the early 1990s economists estimated that the EU internal market would generate between 2.5 and 6.5 per cent extra growth in the European economy.[7] The Commission estimates that in its first ten years, the internal market created 2.5 million jobs and about €5,700 extra income per household in Europe.[8] Also, as companies inside and outside Europe have tried to get a foothold in the new European economy, foreign direct investment flows between and into the EU15 member states increased over eight-fold between 1990 and 2000: from $96bn to $804bn. In contrast, foreign direct investment into the US increased in the same period from only $48bn to $321bn.[9]

Another way to consider the significance of the internal market is the size of the EU economy relative to other economies in the world. Figure 2.2 shows the proportion of total global GDP generated by the EU relative to the US, Japan, India and China. The data illustrate the relative decline of Europe over the last half century. The Chinese economy is already larger than the economies of the original six EU member states, and is rapidly catching up with the collective size of the EU15. The larger EU member states all have smaller economies than China and Japan, and will soon be overtaken by India and more than likely Russia and Brazil. With the growth of global economic integration and the rise of the 'BRIC' economies (Brazil, Russia, China and India), Germany, France, the United Kingdom and Italy are all now 'small states in world markets', as Peter Katzenstein famously described the smaller states in Europe.[10] Without the internal market, the German, French, British and Italian economies would not be large enough to sustain the standards of living which their citizens take for granted without quite radical changes to their existing policy choices.

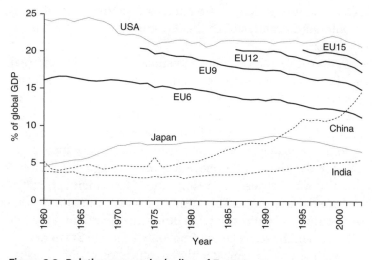

Figure 2.2 Relative economic decline of Europe

Note: EU6 is Belgium, France, Germany, Italy, Luxembourg and the Netherlands. EU9 is the EU6 plus Denmark, Ireland and the United Kingdom. EU12 is the EU9 plus Greece, Portugal and Spain. EU15 is the EU9 plus Austria, Finland and Sweden.

Source: Maddison (2006), author's calculations.

Most of Europe's economic decline relative to the US is a result of lower levels of income growth in Europe in the last twenty years. As a result, in 2003 the GDP per capita of the EU15 states was only 72 per cent of the US level. However, the continuing wealth gap between the US and Europe is explained partly by the different lifestyle choices in Europe and America, where Europeans voluntarily choose to work fewer hours and take longer holidays. So, in 2003, GDP per hour worked in the EU15 was 94 per cent of the US level, and was in fact higher than the US level in France and Italy.[11]

While a significant proportion of the high levels of productivity per hour worked in Europe is explained by domestic factors, economic integration in Europe also played a role, by providing greater economies of scale, lower transactions costs, and more stable public finances. Put this way, without the EU internal market, Europeans could not afford such a luxurious lifestyle!

For sure, there are some economic costs of market integration on a continental scale in Europe. At an individual level, some jobs are lost in underperforming sectors of the economy as a result of competition from more cost-efficient imports, particularly in the tradable sectors of the 'old' member states' economies that were not opened to external competition until the establishment of the internal market.[12] At an aggregate level, there is an inevitable loss of policy-making autonomy as a result of the internal market, the market-correcting and other regulatory policies of the EU, and the areas of national policy that are coordinated at the European level. For example, EU member states are not free to decide independently on the level of market, social and environmental regulation in their national economies, as these are now set largely at the European level. Also, the member states that have joined the Euro have given up having an independent monetary policy, which has traditionally been a major instrument of macro-economic policy. (It is worth pointing out, however, that in a globalising economy the ability to pursue independent micro- and macro-economic policies is limited. For example, the level of economic integration in the Eurozone states prior to the Euro made it almost impossible for these states to pursue independent monetary policies.)

On the other side, the economic benefits of the new architecture in Europe far outweigh the economic costs. At an aggregate level, the internal market has produced economies of scale as a result of gradual industrial integration and rationalisation, higher growth rates than there would be without the internal market, all-time-low inflation rates and interest rates, large transaction cost savings on currency exchange for the states with the Euro, and increasing global economic power for the EU as a whole, which is felt by other states in global trade negotiations and by multinational corporations when they have to comply with the EU regulatory requirements. For example, because of the size of the EU's market in chemicals, the new EU rules on the Registration, Evaluation, and Authorisation of Chemicals (the REACH directive) are likely to become the new global standard, which will have to be adopted by all the other major economies, including the US. As a result of the internal market, the EU is now a policy leader rather than a policy follower, much to the annoyance of some right-wing politicians on the other side of the Atlantic.

Finally, at the individual level, market integration and liberalisation in the internal market have generated countless new jobs and economic opportunities for entrepreneurs. Prices for many goods and services are considerably lower in real economic terms. Citizens take for granted their freedom to travel, work and retire anywhere in the EU. Employees take for granted the opportunities generated by the high levels of foreign direct investment. And, consumers take for granted the new consumption patterns they enjoy in a European-wide market (remember how terrible British supermarkets were in the 1980s compared to today!).

Politics: consensus institutions and shared preferences

Even if economic integration on a continental scale makes sense, how could a continental-scale polity be designed that does not threaten national interests? The political design of the EU, in this regard, is pure genius! The basic operating principle of the EU is 'consensus': meaning that no policies can be adopted without extremely broad political support. This is achieved through multiple checks-and-balances. First, policy powers can only be passed to the European level by unanimous agreement between the EU governments, in reforms of the EU treaties, and after ratification of these agreements by all the member states – either by parliamentary approval or referendum. Second, once a policy area has been passed to the European level, three separate institutions have a say in how EU legislation is made. The European Commission, whose members are appointed by the governments, initiates legislation. Legislation is then amended by the other two institutions: the Council, which is composed of ministers from the EU governments; and the European Parliament, which is composed of politicians who since 1979 have been elected every five years in European-wide elections. In most policy areas, the Council and the Parliament have to adopt identical texts for the legislation to pass. And, in the Council, bills must either pass unanimously, on highly sensitive issues (such as taxation), or must be supported by an oversized majority, via a system of weighted votes known as 'qualified-majority voting' (QMV). Finally, once legislation has been passed by the Council and European Parliament it is subject to judicial review by the European Court of Justice and national courts.

In some respects this design is quite similar to another continental-scale polity: the United States. Both systems have a separation of powers between the executive, legislative and judicial branches of government, which prevents a narrow political majority from dominating policy-making. In both systems smaller states are overrepresented in the legislative process: in the EU in the Commission (where there is one commissioner per member state) and the Council (where voting weights are not purely based on population), and in the US in the Senate (where there are two senators per state). Also, many decisions require supermajorities to pass: a qualified majority in the EU Council, and a three-fifths majority in the

US Senate (where 60 votes out of 100 are needed to break a filibuster).[13]

The positive side of such an institutional design is that policies cannot be adopted unless they are supported by a broad range of political interests. The EU institutional design also ensures that policy outcomes are generally centrist. This is because extremist policies (such as a high level of intervention in the market or radical market liberalisation) are easily blocked by the groups who oppose such a move. On the negative side, though, these checks-and-balances mean that policymaking is difficult and time-consuming, particularly since the enlargement of the EU to twenty-seven states. And once policies have been adopted they are difficult to change, because it only takes a small group of actors to prevent changes to a policy they benefit from, even if a large majority of member states and political parties would prefer a different policy. I return to these problems in the next chapter.

Even with these highly consensual decision-making rules, a political union in Europe is only sustainable because there was a sufficient degree of similarity of policy preferences on the key issues that need to be decided in the creation of a continental-scale economy. The EU internal market was launched in the mid 1980s because of a convergence amongst the member states in their attitudes towards free trade and a liberal market economy. On the right, Margaret Thatcher favoured expanding her domestic privatisation and liberalisation policies to the rest of the EU, via a programme to remove barriers to the movement of goods and services across Europe. The British government was also willing to accept common environmental and some social standards and greater EU expenditure on regional policies as a price for a liberal EU market. On the left, meanwhile, after a failure of his interventionist policies in France in the early 1980s, François Mitterrand supported the creation of a European-wide market to promote European industrial champions who would be able compete with US and Japanese firms, particularly in the high-technology sector.

This consensus is perhaps surprising given the different underlying social and economic models of the EU states. Historically there have been four identifiable models of capitalism in Europe: an Anglo-Saxon model, with deregulated labour markets and relatively low levels of welfare expenditure (in the United Kingdom and Ireland); a Nordic model, with relatively liberal markets and a generous welfare state (in Scandinavia and the Netherlands); a continental model, with regulated labour markets and high level of welfare spending (as in France, Germany and the Benelux); and a Mediterranean model, with regulated labour markets and relatively low levels of welfare spending (as in Spain, Greece and Portugal).[14]

However, this division of Europe into four separate models is highly misleading. The basic socio-economic policies of the EU member states are really quite similar compared to the rest of the world. There has also been a degree of convergence since the 1970s. As figure 2.3 shows, amongst the EU27, most EU member states now have fairly liberal labour markets *and* high levels of public expenditure. Even the United Kingdom, which has traditionally been regarded as an Anglo-Saxon model similar to the United States, has a level of public spending which is closer to the EU average than to the levels in the US, Canada and Australia. There is also likely to be further convergence in the EU, as a result of growing public spending in Ireland, Spain, Slovakia and the Baltic States, as these societies become richer, the gradual liberalisation of labour markets in Germany, Sweden, Finland and Austria, and growing incomes and demands for better public services in the new member states. Essentially, Europe is converging on a new socio-economic model, which is neither the classic Anglo-Saxon model nor the classic continental European model.

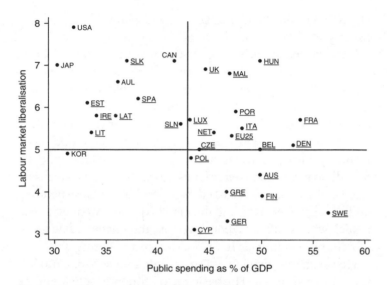

Figure 2.3 One or many European models?

Note: The X-axis is total general government expenditure as a percentage of GDP in 2005. The Y-axis is an index of the degree of liberalisation of a country's labour market, where a higher number means a less regulated labour market, as measured by the Fraser Institute. The lines indicate the average level of public spending in the OECD and the dividing line between low and high levels of labour market liberalisation. The EU member states are underlined.

Sources: Eurostat, OECD and Gwartney *et al.* (2006), authors calculations.

Key for non-EU states:	AUL	Australia	KOR	South Korea
	CAN	Canada	USA	United States
	JAP	Japan		

One could go even further. Despite considerable wealth differences between the states in the enlarged EU, European citizens have remarkably similar basic economic and political values compared to the rest of the world. This is illustrated in figure 2.4, which shows the levels of income inequality in a state and religiosity in the EU and a number of other countries – these two issues are reasonable proxies of public attitudes on the main economic and social issues of modern

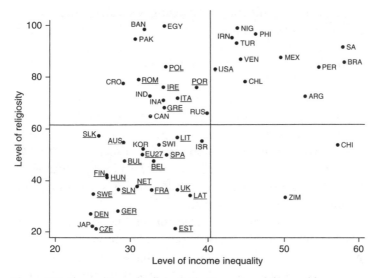

Figure 2.4 Inequality and religiosity in Europe and the world

Note: The X-axis is Gini index of income inequality, where a high number indicates a less equal distribution of wealth in society. The Y-axis is the percentage of citizens who declared that religion plays either a 'rather important' or a 'very important' role in their lives. The lines indicate the global average scores on each scale. The EU member states are underlined (Luxembourg, Cyprus and Malta are not included because of missing data).

Source: World Values Survey, 1999–2004 wave, World Bank 2006 Development Indicators. *Key* for states not in figures 2.1 and 2.3:

ARG	Argentina	IND	India	RUS	Russia
BAN	Bangladesh	IRN	Iran	SA	South Africa
BRA	Brazil	ISR	Israel	SWI	Switzerland
CHI	China	MEX	Mexico	TUR	Turkey
CHL	Chile	NIG	Nigeria	VEN	Venezuela
CRO	Croatia	PAK	Pakistan	ZIM	Zimbabwe
EGY	Egypt	PER	Peru		
INA	Indonesia	PHI	Philippines		

politics. What is striking is how the EU states cluster in the bottom left-hand corner of the figure. Unlike the US, Russia and the developing world (including Turkey!), almost all EU member states are 'post-religious' and have comparatively low levels of income inequality. Growing secularism means that EU states have similar policies on a range of social issues, such as gender equality, the family, abortion and gay marriage. Meanwhile, relatively low levels of income inequality reflect the fact that social democrats have participated in government throughout Europe, and have been able to use their parliamentary majorities (sometimes in coalition with liberals and Christian democrats) to increase public spending on education, housing, welfare, pensions and other social services.[15] As a result of such policies, social mobility is now higher in most EU states than in the US, which is perhaps surprising given the idea of the 'American dream'.

This consensus on basic economic and political values has enabled the EU to adopt a wide range of common policies that go much further than simply correcting potential market failures in a continental-scale economy. These include maximum working hours rules for certain jobs, maternity and paternity leave rights, equal treatment for part-time and temporary workers, requirements that workers' representatives in multi-national firms participate in management decisions, environmental standards relating to the production as well as distribution of goods (whereas a market only needs common rules on the distribution side, such as product standards), a common minimum level of value-added tax, collective spending on humanitarian and development aid, and equal treatment of employees on the grounds of gender, race, ethnicity, religion, age, disability and sexual orientation. In fact, in most of these areas, the EU is more centralised than the US.[16] For example, the US has few federal minimum labour market standards.

In sum, where the political side of European integration is concerned, the checks-and-balances in the design of the EU have meant that sensitive national interests have been protected in the building of a continental-scale economic union.

The need for consensus during this 'polity building' stage has also meant that potential losers from European integration have secured compensation from the potential winners: such as the doubling of regional spending for the periphery states in the late 1980s, who felt that they were less likely to benefit from the internal market than the core exporting economies. Also, with this consensus, although there is certainly a loss of political sovereignty in the EU as a result of passing policy-making powers to the European level, the risk that a major decision would go against any particular member state was small. But, even with such consensus-promoting institutions, shared social and economic values in Europe have enabled the EU to adopt a wide range of common policies beyond simply creation and integration of the internal market.

Conclusion: the EU is a remarkable achievement . . . but could be even better

In the early twentieth century, Europe suffered the two most destructive wars in human history, as the culmination of centuries of rivalries between the states of Europe. At the beginning of the twenty-first century, in contrast, the states of Eastern and Western Europe are united in a continental-scale political system, where specific executive, legislative and judicial powers have been passed to the European level to allow a continent-wide market to be created and governed. This would have been unimaginable for my grandparents' generation while they were living through the bombing of London in the 1940s, experiencing the economic hardships of the immediate post-war period, and witnessing the start of the Cold War in the 1950s. Yet, half a century later, the EU internal market guarantees the economic prosperity of almost half a billion people, the EU adopts common policies in a wide range of areas that extend the economic and political rights of European citizens, and most EU citizens take for granted the employment, investment, consumption, educational, travel, social and lifestyle opportunities they now have because of the EU. Above all, for the first time in human history, a war between the major states of Europe is almost unimaginable. Put in these terms, the EU is one of the most remarkable political achievements of the modern age.

Some anti-European politicians argue that global economic integration could be a substitute for European economic integration. Who needs a continental-scale market, they claim, if a global market could provide even greater specialisation and economies of scale? However, such claims are delusional. The fundamental difference between the EU and global economic integration is on the political side. Without a much higher level of convergence on basic social and political values on a global scale, a world community will not be able to adopt the necessary market correcting measures to allow a genuine global single market to function. For example, agreement on basic global emissions standards and core labour standards is extremely difficult, and global standards on the equal treatment of men and women in the workplace are virtually unthinkable. As a result, it is extremely unlikely that global economic integration will develop much beyond the removal of trade barriers in a subset of products and services. With the EU internal market and now the Euro, economic integration in Europe is of a wholly different magnitude, and the benefits of this greater degree of economic integration have only been possible because European citizens share some basic values about how economic and social relations should be organised and regulated.

Nonetheless, the EU could be even better. Now that the basic economic and political architecture of the European-scale polity has been built, the EU faces some tough decisions. For example, the service sector needs to be far more integrated, to maximise economies of scale and economic opportunities in the fastest growing sector of the modern economy. The energy market needs to be better integrated and organised, to address the chronic problem of Europe's energy dependency on outside states. Europe needs a more effective policy to tackle climate change. Europe needs policies that help promote genuinely free movement of persons in Europe and to integrate minorities in the new multiethnic European society. And, Europe needs policies and actions to protect its interests and project its values on the world stage. In all these areas, action is needed at the European level rather than just at the national level. Yet, the EU is unlikely to be able to meet these challenges because of its political architecture: which makes policy change extremely difficult and which does not allow citizens much influence over the direction of EU policy. Having made the case for the EU, how the EU could be better is the subject of the rest of this book.

PART I

The Diagnosis

CHAPTER THREE

Policy gridlock

The EU needs to face up to several important policy challenges. One key challenge is reform of the European economy, to enable Europe to remain competitive in the new global economy. Some aspects of economic reform can only be addressed at the national level, such as changes to pensions systems, the welfare state and labour markets. Nevertheless, several key elements of economic reform need to be addressed at the European level, such as liberalisation and integration of the services and energy sectors, establishment of a genuine internal market in financial services, reform of agricultural subsidies and reform of some of the EU's social regulations, which impose a significant regulatory burden on small and medium-sized enterprises.[1] The EU is currently unable to make these changes because it suffers from 'policy gridlock'.

It is often assumed that the main reason for this gridlock is the design of the EU institutions, which forces decisions to be made by a broad consensus amongst the member states and the EU institutions. Consensus is certainly more difficult to reach now that the EU has twenty-seven member states. However, contrary to popular wisdom, the institutional design of the EU is not the main reason for the gridlock. With the reforms of the EU treaties in the last twenty years, the EU institutions are now far less consensus oriented than they used to be.

The main reason for gridlock is that the policy agenda of the EU has shifted, from creating the internal market to economic reform. During the period of building the internal market, between the mid 1980s and mid 1990s, the EU was able to pass a large amount of legislation because there was overwhelming support for changes to existing policies. In contrast, since the late 1990s the EU has been less able to make policy changes because EU leaders have wanted to change policies in opposite directions: with some supporting more EU social regulations and others supporting more economic liberalisation.

This chapter elaborates this argument. I first explain how the recent treaty changes have moved the EU away from a hyper-consensus form of government towards a more majoritarian form of government. I then look at the primary cause of gridlock: the shift in the policy agenda from the creation of the internal market to economic reform.

Evolution of the EU from consensual to partially majoritarian government

Political scientists often use a majoritarian-consensual continuum to understand how different models of government work, where the more majoritarian a political system is, the easier it will be to change policies.[2] At the majoritarian extreme are systems where a single party with a narrow majority can dominate decision-making (as is usually the case in Britain). At the consensual extreme are systems where a large coalition is needed for policies to be changed. This could be because a large coalition government is the norm or because one party controls the executive while another holds a majority in the legislature (as is often the case in the US).

For most of its existence the EU has been at the consensual extreme of this continuum, where a broad coalition of member states and political parties was required to get anything done. However, three major reforms in the last two decades have made the EU more majoritarian and less consensual: (1) the extension of qualified-majority voting in the Council; (2) the

Table 3.1 Qualified-majority voting in the EU Council		
	Votes	Probability of being pivotal
France, Germany, Italy, United Kingdom	29	0.087
Poland, Spain	27	0.080
Romania	14	0.040
Netherlands	13	0.037
Belgium, Czech Republic, Greece, Hungary, Portugal	12	0.034
Austria, Bulgaria, Sweden	10	0.028
Denmark, Finland, Ireland, Lithuania, Slovakia	7	0.020
Cyprus, Estonia, Latvia, Luxembourg, Slovenia	4	0.011
Malta	3	0.008
Total votes	345	
Votes needed to adopt a decision	255 (73.9%)	
Votes needed to block a decision	91 (26.4%)	

Under the rules of the Nice Treaty, as amended by the Accession Treaties with Bulgaria and Romania, a 'triple majority' is required, of 255 out of 345 for 27 member states, a majority of member states, and 62% of the population of the member states. The Bräuninger and König (2001) programme was used to calculate the probability of being pivotal.

increases in the legislative powers of the European Parliament; and (3) the changes to the way the European Commission is chosen.

Table 3.1 shows how QMV works in the Council. Put simply, the larger member states have more votes than the smaller member states and decisions require almost 74 per cent of the votes to pass. Formally, as well as commanding 255 of the 345 votes, a qualified majority must also represent a majority of the member states and 62 per cent of the EU population. In practice, however, a coalition that commands almost 74 per cent of the votes almost certainly also contains a majority of the states who together have 62 per cent of the population.

On the one hand, the QMV threshold is more than a simple majority (of 50 per cent plus 1 votes). This means that a relatively broad coalition is still required for most decisions in the Council. On the other hand, 74 per cent is a lot easier to achieve than a unanimous agreement between all the member states, which was the norm in almost all policy areas until the mid 1980s.[3]

Successive reforms have extended QMV to a wide range of policy areas. This began with the Single European Act in 1987, which introduced QMV for most issues relating to the creation of the internal market. The Maastricht Treaty in 1993 then extended QMV in most areas of social and environmental policy. The Amsterdam Treaty in 1999 further extended QMV in the area of social policy. And the Nice Treaty in 2003 extended QMV in the area of justice and interior affairs. As table 3.2 consequently shows, most of the main areas relating to the liberalisation and regulation of the movement of goods, services, capital and labour in the European economy are now subject to QMV in the Council. Only highly sensitive issues, such as taxation, social security provisions and internal border controls remain under unanimity.

The second major set of institutional changes relate to the European Parliament's powers. Prior to the Single European Act the European Parliament was only a consultative body. Today, the European Parliament is one of the most powerful legislative chambers in the world. The Single European Act gave the European Parliament two readings of most legislation in the creation of the internal market and made it difficult for the Council to overturn amendments proposed by the Parliament. The Maastricht Treaty introduced the 'co-decision procedure', and the Amsterdam Treaty reformed and extended the procedure to cover almost all areas of legislation where QMV is used in the Council. Under the co-decision procedure, the Commission has the sole right to propose legislation. The

Table 3.2 Main policies covered by qualified-majority voting and unanimity

EU policies requiring QMV	EU policies requiring Unanimity
Free movement of goods, services, capital and labour in the internal market	
Removal of technical and physical barriers	Consumption, corporate and personal taxes
Free movement and residence of workers	
Mutual recognition of qualifications	
Common customs tariff	
Liberalisation of services	
Free movement of capital	
State aids and prevention of distortion of competition	
Economic and monetary union	
Economic policy guidelines	Enforcement of Stability and Growth Pact
General orientations for exchange rate policy	Exchange rate agreements with non-EU currencies
International currency agreements	Appointment of ECB officials
Environmental and social policies	
General environment policies	Environmental taxes
Equal pay and treatment of men and women	Non-discrimination on grounds of sex, race, ethnicity religion, disability, age or sexual orientation
Working conditions	Protection of workers whose contracts are terminated
Health and safety at work	Social security
Information and consultation of workers	Conditions of employment for third-country nationals
Integration of persons excluded from the labour market	
Modernisation of social protection systems	

Table 3.2 *(cont.)*	
EU policies requiring QMV	EU policies requiring Unanimity
Budgetary policies	
Adoption of the annual EU budget	Adoption of the multiannual EU budget
Operation of the Common Agricultural Policy	
Regional funds	
Research and development spending	
Justice and interior affairs	
Checks at external borders	Internal border controls
Asylum, visas and movement of third-country nationals	Extradition policy
Implementation of police and judicial cooperation measures	Adoption of police and judicial cooperation measures
Judicial cooperation in civil matters	
Common Foreign and Security Policy (CFSP) and external economic policies	
Implementation of CFSP joint actions	CFSP joint actions
Common Commercial Policy (CCP)	Extend CCP to intellectual property and services
Negotiation of international trade agreements	Conclusion of international trade agreements
Development cooperation	
Other Provisions	
Suspend rights of a member state	Declare that a member state has breached EU principles
	Adoption of any measure not covered in the Treaty

European Parliament and the Council then each have two readings of the legislation, and if the Council and the European Parliament still disagree a 'conciliation committee' is convened, with an equal number of delegates from the two

chambers. As a result, under the main EU legislative procedure legislation cannot be adopted unless it is supported by a
qualified majority in the Council as well as a simple majority in
the European Parliament.

Because of the power of the European Parliament under the
co-decision procedure and because this procedure now covers
a wide range of EU policies, the European Parliament is now
more powerful than most national parliaments in Europe.
National parliaments have very little legislative power. This is
because they are dominated by governments, who command a
majority in parliament and can use a variety of carrots and
sticks to force their backbenchers to support government bills
(such as the promise of promotion to ministerial office or the
threat of a vote of confidence and early elections). One British
backbencher once described his life in parliament as 'throwing
paper aeroplanes at the government bulldozer'.[4]

In contrast, the majority in the European Parliament is fully
independent from both the Commission and the Council. The
European Parliament cannot be dissolved by the Commission
or the Council, and there are no ministerial carrots the
Commission can offer the MEPs. Because of this independence from the Commission and Council, the European
Parliament has been able to block several significant pieces of
legislation and has been able to force the Commission and the
Council to accept more than 50 per cent of its amendments to
legislation.[5]

The third major change is the way the European Commission
is appointed. Until the Maastricht Treaty, the Commission pres
ident was chosen unanimously by the EU governments and the
other members of the Commission were then nominated by
each government and approved by a unanimous vote in the
European Council (of the EU heads of government). The
European Parliament had no formal role in this process until
the Maastricht Treaty, which allowed the European Parliament

to be 'consulted' on the choice of Commission President and to veto the Commission as a whole. The European Parliament interpreted this right to be consulted as a formal right of veto, which was reluctantly accepted by the governments.[6] This *de facto* right of the European Parliament to 'elect' the candidate proposed by the governments was then formalised in the Amsterdam Treaty.

The Nice Treaty then introduced the rule that the Commission President and the Commission as a whole would be proposed by the European Council by QMV rather than unanimity. At face value this reform may seem fairly innocuous. In reality, however, this is a fundamental change, as it means that the same-sized majority in the Council and Parliament is now needed to elect the Commission and pass the legislative proposals of the Commission. This means that the EU is now a quasi-parliamentary system of government – where a particular political majority could choose 'their' Commission with a particular policy agenda and so be 'in government' at the EU level for a particular period, while several member states and some political parties could find themselves 'in opposition'.

The effect of the introduction of QMV in the Nice Treaty for electing the Commission was immediately apparent in the election of the 2005–9 Commission. Several candidates for the Commission President put their names on the table. The French and German governments backed the liberal Belgian prime minister, Guy Verhofstadt. However, after it became clear that José Manuel Durão Barroso, the Portuguese centre-right prime minister, had sufficient support to reach the QMV threshold, the French and German governments backed down. Barroso was then supported by a centre-right majority in the vote in the European Parliament, with many MEPs on the centre-left and extreme-left voting against him.

The anti-Barroso MEPs then added the support of the liberal MEPs in opposing the appointment of Rocco Buttiglione, an

Italian Christian democrat, as the justice and home affairs com-missioner. This portfolio included EU legislation on women's rights and non-discrimination on the grounds of sexual orienta-tion, which were issues on which Buttiglione had rather extreme views. The liberal-left coalition represented a majority in the Parliament and so threatened to block the appointment of the Commission as a whole (as the European Parliament cannot veto single commissioners). This forced Barroso to withdraw the slate of commissioners only minutes before the vote on 27 October 2004. One reason the anti-Buttiglione coalition held together was that the German socialist and French conservative governments, who had been on the losing side in the European Council in the nomination of Barroso, had no incentive to lobby their MEPs to support the Commission in the Parliament. In the end, Buttiglione was replaced and the Barroso Commission was elected by a narrow centre-right majority in both the European Council and Parliament.

Put together, these three sets of treaty changes have funda-mentally altered the design of the EU. The EU originally had a highly consensual system of government, where intergov-ernmental deals in the Council were required for all major decisions, which allowed each government a veto on anything they did not like. The EU now has a much more majoritarian set of institutions. A particular political coalition – albeit one that would have to be broad enough to command qualified-majority support in the Council as well as a majority in the European Parliament – now has the potential to choose its own Commission President and Commission and also enact policy proposals that are opposed by a minority of govern-ments in the Council and political parties in the European Parliament. In other words, the reason the EU has failed to make crucial policy changes in the last few years has very little to do with the institutional design of the EU. The EU should be much more able to undertake policy reforms after the recent treaty changes than under the original highly consensual institutions. The reason the EU suffers from policy gridlock lies elsewhere, in the shifting policy agenda of the EU.

Shifting policy agenda: from market building to economic reform

The policy agenda of the EU has shifted from a focus on the creation of the internal market to reform of existing economic and social policies at the national and European levels.[7] To understand how this change has caused policy gridlock I need to introduce some simple ideas from political science about how policy-making works. First, on any policy issue, decision-making involves replacing an existing policy, called a 'status quo policy', with a new policy. Second, each actor in the policy process – such as a government in the Council, a political party in the European Parliament, and the Commission – has a clear 'preference' about which policy they would like to see adopted. Third, the difference between these preferences and the status quo policy determines the range of policies that could replace the status quo policy. Fourth, which particular policy in this range will be adopted depends on which actor has the power to make the initial proposal (to be the agenda-setter) and which actor has the power to block a proposal. In the EU, the Commission has agenda-setting power, as it has a monopoly on legislative initiative, and the government in the Council that is pivotal in turning a losing qualified majority into a winning qualified majority has the blocking power.

An example helps illustrate the intuitions that derive from these simple ideas. Before the creation of the internal market there were no common EU environmental packaging standards. The Scandinavian governments wanted the EU to adopt quite restrictive packaging standards whereas some Southern European governments wanted less restrictive standards.

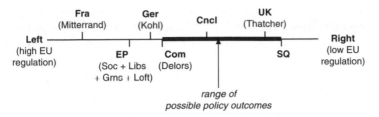

Figure 3.1 Policy change in the creation of the internal market, mid 1980s to mid 1990s

Notes: SQ location of the status quo policy; Com location of the Commission; Cncl location of the winning coalition in the Council under qualified-majority voting; EP location of the winning coalition in the European Parliament

However, all governments wanted common EU packaging standards because these were essential for the internal market to operate. So, when the Commission proposed relatively high environmental packaging standards, even the Southern European governments were willing to vote for them rather than the policy status quo (of no free movement of goods in the internal market).

In fact, this was generally how EU policy-making worked in the period of the creation of the internal market in the mid 1980s to the mid 1990s. This is illustrated in figure 3.1. The main dimension of policy-making in this period was the level of EU regulation in the internal market, with some states wanting less EU regulation and others wanting more EU regulation. Because the EU had no common standards prior to the internal market, the existing policy (SQ) was at the 'low regulation' extreme of this dimension. Governments on the left generally preferred higher consumer, environmental and social standards while governments on the right generally preferred 'lighter touch regulation' in the internal market. Of the three largest member states, the French socialist president, François Mitterrand, advocated a 'social dimension' to the internal market programme, and was largely supported in this agenda by Helmut Kohl's Christian democratic-liberal coalition in Germany. At the other extreme, Margaret Thatcher's conservative government in Britain supported the internal market but adamantly opposed EU social regulations – 'we did not roll back the state in London to have it re-imposed through the backdoor from Brussels', as she famously put it. Thatcher was marginalised, however, as the qualified-majority coalition in the Council was relatively centrist, as was the Delors Commission, and the European Parliament was dominated by a centre-left coalition of socialists, liberals, greens and radical left MEPs (particularly in the 1989 to 1994 period).

As a result of the position of the status quo policy and the line-up of the actors relative to this status quo there was a very wide range of policies that could be adopted by the EU in this period. For example, the Commission was able to propose a relatively high level of environmental protection which was supported by a qualified majority in the Council and the majority in the European Parliament. The British government often opposed these policies, but risked being defeated. Similarly, the Commission proposed moderate health and safety standards in the internal market which even the British government supported, as Thatcher was rather indifferent between a moderate level of health and safety regulation and the existing status quo policy (of not having a functioning internal market).

The move from unanimity to QMV after the Single European Act, and increasing the powers of the European Parliament, certainly had some impact. However, the key thing to understand about the internal market project is that the reason the EU was able to pass more than 300 pieces of legislation in this period was that there was a very large range of policies that all the key actors were willing to accept since the alternative, of not having a working internal market in a wide range of goods and services, was so undesirable.

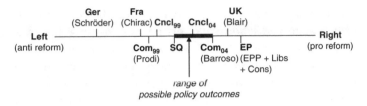

Figure 3.2 Policy gridlock on economic and social reform, late 1990s
to the present

Notes: SQ location of the status quo policy; Com_{99}, Com_{04} location of the
European Commission in 1999 and 2004; $Cncl_{99}$, $Cncl_{04}$ location of the
winning coalition in the Council under qualified-majority voting in 1999 and
2004; EP location of the winning coalition in the European Parliament

The situation from the late 1990s to the present is very different, as figure 3.2 shows. As discussed, there were some
important institutional changes between the earlier period and
this period. QMV was extended to a wider set of policies by the
Maastricht and Amsterdam treaties and the powers of the
European Parliament were increased with the introduction of
the co-decision procedure. However, the institutions were not
really so different from the earlier period, as the Single
European Act had already established QMV in the Council for
most of the key areas for creating and regulating the internal
market and introduced two readings in the European
Parliament for most internal market legislation.

The key change between the two periods was the nature of
the policy agenda. Whereas in the mid 1980s to mid 1990s the
main issue was the creation of the internal market, since the
late 1990s the main issue has been how regulated or liberalised the internal market should be. On this new set of issues,
Gerhard Schröder's 'red-green' coalition was furthest to the
left of the three largest member states, opposing any attempt to
further liberalise the basic internal market rules (as in German
opposition to the Takeover Directive). French president

Jacques Chirac was a conservative, but on the reform of the welfare state and labour markets he was closer to the traditional socialists than social democrat modernisers such as Wim Kok or Tony Blair. The Blair government, meanwhile, was on the centre-right on EU economic reform issues: supporting liberal reforms (such as the Takeover Directive) and opposing new social regulations (such as the Working Time Directive). The qualified-majority coalition in the Council changed between 1999 and 2004. Whereas in 1999 there was a clear majority in the Council on the centre-left, by 2004 many of these governments had been replaced by centre-right parties.

The changing make-up of the Council was reflected in the changing make-up of the Commission, since the governments choose the commissioners. The 1999–2004 Prodi Commission had a centre-left majority while the 2004–9 Barroso Commission had a centre-right majority. Meanwhile, after the 1999 European elections the European Parliament was dominated by a centre-right coalition, with the European People's Party (EPP), of Christian democrats and conservatives, replacing the Party of European Socialists (PES) as the largest party group, and supported on most economic reform issues by the liberal group, which is the third largest group and sits between the EPP and the PES.

Nevertheless, the most significant change between the earlier and later period was in the location of existing policy status quos. In the creation of the internal market, virtually all actors preferred any EU legislation to the status quo (of no internal market). By the late 1990s, in contrast, most policy issues involved reforming an existing set of relatively centrist policies. In this new situation, some governments and parties wanted to move existing policies leftwards, for example by adopting new social regulations or by harmonising company taxes, while others wanted to move existing policies rightwards, for example by liberalising takeover provisions, the labour markets and the service sector.

This meant that the range of existing policies that a qualified majority in the Council and a majority in the European Parliament could agree was now rather small. For example, under the Prodi Commission, where the majorities in the Commission and Council were on the left and the majority in the European Parliament was on the right, agreement between the Council and the European Parliament was all but impossible, since the coalition in the European Parliament favoured liberalising existing economic policies, while the coalition in the Council and Commission favoured more EU regulation. The EU was truly 'gridlocked' in this period.

This resulted in several high-profile battles between the institutions under the Prodi Commission. For example, on the End-of-Life Vehicle Directive, the Commission proposed a highly regulatory set of common standards for the recycling of cars, where the costs would be borne largely by the car manufacturers. This position was supported by a green-left majority in the Council in July 1999. The new centre-right majority in the post-1999 European Parliament then watered-down the proposed legislation, for example by allowing more discretion in the implementation of the legislation by each government. A deal was eventually struck between the Council and European Parliament, which largely accepted the existing informal practices that existed in most member states – in other words the existing status quo policy for most member states.

When Barroso was elected in 2004 it at first seemed that reform would now be possible because the centre-right majorities in the Commission, the Council and the European Parliament were all on the 'pro reform' side of the status quo policy. Realising this window of opportunity, Barroso set out a reformist agenda in the Commission's 2005 work programme, which was endorsed by a narrow majority in the

European Parliament, with most socialist, green and radical-left MEPs voting against. But, the reform agenda immediately stalled, as the battle over the Services Directive revealed.[8]

The Barroso Commission supported a relatively liberal Services Directive, based around the 'country-of-origin' principle. This principle meant that if a service provider was registered in his or her home member state he or she could not be prevented from providing services anywhere in the EU. This principle immediately came under attack from the French and German governments and many left-wing MEPs, who argued that such a principle would undermine the high social standards that applied to most services in some member states. In the end, the new Christian democrat–social democratic government in Germany brokered a deal between the two largest parties in the European Parliament (who were both led by German politicians).[9] This deal replaced the country-of-origin principle with a weaker principle of the 'freedom to provide services' and derogations for many key sectors. The deal was amended in a more liberal direction in the first reading of the legislation in the European Parliament, which was then backed by a qualified majority in the Council. The result was a Services Directive that is not as reformist as the Commission had originally proposed, although it was a moderate move 'rightwards' from the existing status quo policy.

In general, then, the shift in the policy agenda from creating the internal market to how liberal or regulated the internal market should be has meant that policy-making at the European level is much more difficult and prone to lowest-common-denominator outcomes than it used to be. As figure 3.3 shows, the volume of legislative acts adopted by the EU dramatically declined between the late 1980s and the early 2000s. Part of this decline is explained by the fact that the EU has had less to do after the high volume of legislation needed to create the internal market prior to 31 December 1992. However,

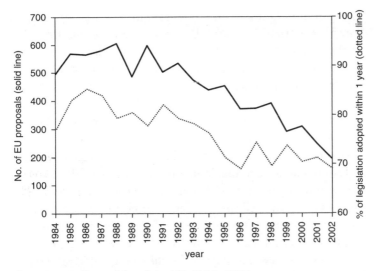

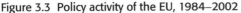

Figure 3.3 Policy activity of the EU, 1984–2002

Source: Author's calculations from dataset used in König et al. (2006).

another reason for the decline is that the Commission has reacted to the fact that it is simply harder to reach an agreement. This effect is shown by the decline in the proportion of legislation that is adopted within one year of its proposal by the Commission (the dotted line in the figure).

Conclusion: the need for a political mandate not institutional reform

In sum, the EU suffers from severe policy gridlock. It is extremely difficult to get things done at the European level, and most new EU policies are extremely watered-down deals that hardly change existing European or national provisions. What is striking, though, is that this new gridlock is not the fault of the design of the EU institutions. The extension of

QMV in the Council, the increase in the powers of the European Parliament, and the new rules for electing the Commission, mean that the EU is now much less consensual than it used to be. But, as the EU system of government has become more majoritarian, which should theoretically make policy change easier, policy-making at the European level has become more difficult. So, the institutional design of the EU cannot be the cause of gridlock.

The reason the EU is so incapable of acting effectively is the shift in the policy agenda. While the main aim of the EU was the creation of the internal market, policy-making was relatively easy because all the key actors preferred the creation of the internal market and some level of common market regulation to no internal market. Now the EU has turned to the issue of how far the internal market should be regulated or deregulated, the picture is radically different. Any change to existing policies would lead to some governments and parties winning (as policies move towards their preferred positions) and others losing (as policies move further from their preferred positions). As a result, it is extremely difficult for a coalition to be built between the Commission, Council and European Parliament that can enact policy reforms.

Sure, the EU decision-making system could be made more efficient, for example with a single president of the European Council rather than the current six-monthly rotating presidency or with a reduction in the threshold needed for QMV in the Council. However, these reforms are rather insignificant relative to the major institutional reforms that were brought about by the Single European Act and the Maastricht, Amsterdam and Nice treaties. And the main cause of the policy gridlock would remain: the problem of how to reform existing policies when one group of governments and parties want policy change in one direction while another group wants policy change in the opposite direction.

There is some hope. The institutional changes would allow a majority coalition to undertake reforms if the coalitions in the Commission, Council and European Parliament were all on the same side. However, the first time the EU experienced such 'unified government', in 2005, policy-making immediately stalled. This was not a fault of the institutions nor a fault of the location of the policy status quo, as the centre-right majorities in all three of the EU institutions supported the Barroso Commission's economic reform agenda. The problem was a lack of a sufficient mandate for Barroso's reform package. The main government on the minority side of this situation, the French government, questioned the legitimacy of the agenda pursued by the new majorities in the Commission, Council and European Parliament. France could have been outvoted (as it had been in the election of Barroso as Commission President), but France was due to hold a referendum on the EU Constitution, which forced the Commission and the governments to water down any reforms.

So, in general, policy-making is now very difficult, although the EU institutions would allow policy change under certain specific conditions. But, when a window of opportunity to undertake reforms opened up, as it did in 2005, the EU lacked a legitimate mandate to make any major changes that would be against the interests of any of the big players. Why the EU lacks this legitimacy is the subject of the next chapter.

CHAPTER FOUR

Lack of popular legitimacy

In the space of four days in the Spring of 2005, the citizens of two of the founding EU member states rejected the EU Constitution; with 55 per cent voting No in France on 29 May and 62 per cent voting No in the Netherlands on 1 June. The French referendum was always likely to be close, given the unpopularity of President Chirac and the divisions on the Constitution in the French socialist party. What was perhaps more shocking for the EU establishment was the size of the No vote in the Netherlands. Dutch citizens had for a long time been amongst the most enthusiastic supporters of European integration, yet they voted almost two-to-one against the Constitution.

Many commentators dismissed these two outcomes as largely unrelated to the EU – as an anti-Chirac backlash in France and a symptom of a continuing malaise in Dutch politics after the dramatic rise and then murder of Pim Fortuyn. However, this understanding of the outcome in these two referendums is largely wrong. Research has revealed that citizens' attitudes towards the EU were far stronger predictors of how people voted in France and the Netherlands (as well as in the votes in Spain and Luxembourg) than any other factor, such as whether a citizen supported or opposed the government, which party he or she supported, or whether he or she was on the left or the right.[1]

In the last decade there has been a dramatic transformation in public attitudes towards the EU. Had the collapse in underlying attitudes towards the EU not been so great, the EU Constitution would have been ratified in all the member states. Fifteen years ago European citizens used to trust their governments to represent their interests in Brussels. Today, the majority of citizens in all member states are not committed to the 'European project' and so do not blindly accept European-level deals done by their governments. Scholars of public opinion have been warning for some time that public attitudes towards the EU are a 'ticking bomb'.[2] In the Spring of 2005 this bomb finally went off.

I do two things in this chapter: first, I demonstrate that there has been a dramatic collapse in the popular legitimacy of the EU since the early 1990s; and, second, I look at what factors shape support and opposition towards the EU today, to understand what the EU might do to increase support in the future. The main argument is that the EU is now in a fundamentally new political context, with a worryingly low level of popular support, which may fall even further. Procedural changes in the way the EU works, such as increases in the powers of the European Parliament, greater transparency of EU decisions, involving interest groups and national parliaments in EU decision-making, and the Charter of Fundamental Rights, have all failed to engage citizens in EU politics. The political elites need to think about how to address the legitimacy problem in more substantive ways, and quickly.

The rise and fall of public support for the EU

Since the early 1970s Eurobarometer opinion polls have been conducted every six months in all the EU member states. These polls are funded from the EU budget, but are conducted by private and well-respected polling agencies in each country. As a result, the Eurobarometer polls provide a rich source of data for tracking and understanding public support for European integration as well as numerous other political and social attitudes of European citizens.

One question which has been asked in every Eurobarometer survey since the beginning is: 'Generally speaking, do you think [your country's] membership of the European Community/ Union is a good thing, a bad thing, neither good nor bad, or don't know?' This question is simple for citizens to understand, is more concrete than abstract questions about support for 'European integration' or 'European identity', and so has become the standard question to measure support for the EU across countries and over time.

Figure 4.1 shows the percentage of EU citizens who thought that their county's membership of the EU was a 'good thing' in each year over the last two decades.[3] In the late 1970s almost 60 per cent of citizens supported EU membership. There was then a rise in support in the late 1980s, which peaked around 1991, when over 70 per cent of citizens supported member-ship. This was followed by an equally steep decline until about 1996. Since then, public support has remained fairly stable. The worrying thing, though, is the absolute level of support for EU membership in the last decade, which has hovered at or just above 50 per cent. In other words, only about half of all EU citizens think their country's membership of the EU is a good thing. The other half are either opposed to EU membership or indifferent. This is an extremely low level of support for a polit-ical organisation, and is hardly a strong basis upon which to undertake European-level policy reforms which might pro-duce winners and losers (as discussed in the previous chapter).

One popular view is that support for the EU is a 'fair-weather phenomenon', meaning that citizens like European integra-tion when the economy is booming and dislike European inte-gration when the economy is declining – either because they blame the EU for the lack of economic success or because they want their national governments to protect them from compe-tition from other member states.[4] As figure 4.1 shows, before the early 1990s, support for the EU and economic growth went

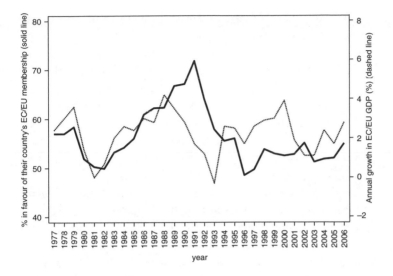
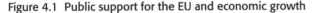

Figure 4.1 Public support for the EU and economic growth

Source: Author's calculations from Eurobarometer survey data and Eurostat.

hand in hand: with support declining with the second oil crisis in the early 1980s and rising as the European economy picked up in the mid 1980s. Since 1987, however, the relationship has changed. Support for the EU continued to rise until 1991, despite the fact that economic growth slowed down after 1987. Economic growth then started to pick up in 1993 and rose until 2000, while public support for the EU moved in the opposite direction in this period: falling almost 10 percentage points.

What happened is that citizens started to notice that the EU had become far more than simply an economic union. There was initial enthusiasm for the creation of the internal market, and the belief that 'Europe 1992' would usher in a new era of economic and social opportunities for Europeans. Popular opposition to the EU then emerged during the ratification of the Maastricht Treaty in 1992 and 1993. The Danish public voted against the Maastricht Treaty in a referendum in June 1992, the French public only narrowly voted in favour of the treaty in September 1992, the British government was defeated on the treaty in the House of Commons, and there was a challenge to the treaty in the German Constitutional Court, which ruled that the treaty could be ratified but set some restrictive conditions for any future treaty reforms. Norway then voted against joining the EU in 1994, and the 1994 European elections saw Eurosceptic parties gain votes in several member states.

Until the launch of the internal market and the establishment of the 'European Union' by the Maastricht Treaty, most European citizens knew very little about the EU. From the mid 1990s onwards, information about the EU has been more readily available, EU meetings and decisions have been more prominent in TV news and newspapers, and public understanding of the EU has grown as a result. This has meant that most citizens now form their own judgements about the costs and benefits of the EU, rather than simply accepting the claims of their governments. As Franklin, Marsh and McLaren elegantly put it in 1994: the anti-Europe 'bottle' had been 'uncorked'.[5]

A constitution for the EU was at least partially conceived as an attempt to address these public concerns. When the Convention on the Future of Europe, which drafted the Constitution, was launched at the Laeken European Council in December 2001 the EU heads of government declared that 'the European institutions must be brought closer to its [sic] citizens'.[6] But, this attempt dramatically backfired. Had the French and Dutch not rejected the Constitution, the Constitution would almost certainly have been defeated in at least one and potentially all of the planned or likely referendums in the United Kingdom, Poland, the Czech Republic, Denmark, Sweden, Ireland and Portugal.

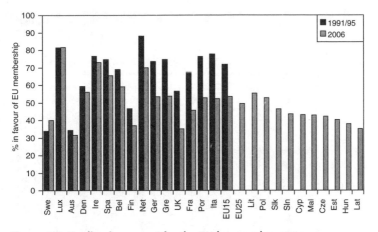

Figure 4.2 Decline in support for the EU by member state

Note: For the 'old 15' member states, the graph shows the levels of support for EU membership in 1991 and 2006, except for Sweden, Austria and Finland, where the comparison is between 1995 and 2006. The 'old15' member states are sorted from the lowest decline in support (on the furthest left) to the highest decline in support (on the furthest right). The 'new10' are sorted between the highest and lowest levels of support in 2006.

Source: Author's calculations from Eurobarometer 35 (Spring 1991), 43 (Spring 1995), and 66 (Autumn 2006) survey data.

The low level of public support for the EU hides considerable variations between the member states, as figure 4.2 shows. At one extreme, in the United Kingdom, Sweden, Austria, Finland, Latvia, Hungary and Estonia less than 40 per cent of citizens are in favour of EU membership. At the other extreme, in Luxembourg, Ireland and the Netherlands more than 70 per cent of citizens are in favour of EU membership. What is striking, though, is the extent of the decline in support for the EU in some of the traditionally EU-enthusiast countries. For example, although the absolute level of support remains comparatively high in the Netherlands, there has been an almost 20 per cent fall in Dutch support in the last

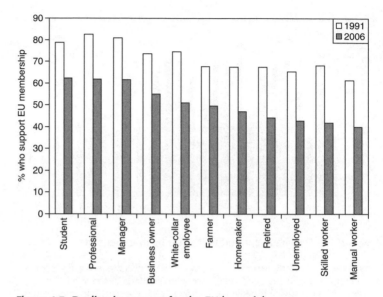

Figure 4.3 Decline in support for the EU by social group

Source: Author's calculations from Eurobarometer 35 (Spring 1991) and 66 (Autumn 2006) survey data.

fifteen years, and an even greater decline in Germany and France. And, perhaps most strikingly, Italy used to be the first or second most pro-European member state, but since 1991 there has been a 25 per cent decline in the percentage of Italians who think Italian membership of the EU is a good thing. As a result, some Italian political parties and newspaper editors are now openly hostile towards the EU, for example suggesting that Italy should withdraw from economic and monetary union.

Furthermore, whereas there are some variations across countries, the extent of the decline in public support for the EU is similar across social groups, as figure 4.3 shows. People in 'higher' social groups, who are employed in more highly skilled positions, are more supportive of the EU than people in 'lower' social groups, who are employed in less highly skilled positions. So, professionals, managers, business owners and students (who presumably expect to enter a highly skilled occupation) support the EU more than skilled or manual workers, the unemployed or the retired. However, the decline in public support in the last fifteen years across all social groups means that professionals, managers and business owners are less supportive of the EU today than skilled or manual workers were in 1991.

In sum, there has been a remarkable decline in public support for the EU in the last decade or so. The absolute level of support for the EU is now extremely low, at around 50 per cent of the population. Citizens in even the original six member states are increasingly anti-European. Given these trends, the results of the referendums in France and the Netherlands were much more predictable than most EU insiders realised. The unpopularity of the French and Dutch governments in 2005 certainly played a part in the referendum defeats. However, the powerful trends in public attitudes against Europe suggest that it is simply wrong to dismiss these votes as driven by factors completely unrelated to the EU.

'Why don't they like us?' Understanding public attitudes towards the EU today

Given the weak popular legitimacy of the EU, one of the most important questions facing Europe's leaders is what can be done to increase public support for Europe? To answer this question we need to understand why some people like the EU and some people hate it. A useful way of thinking about this is to use an established set of ideas in political science about what determines support for political institutions.[7] These ideas were originally developed by David Easton to explain variations in the legitimacy of national institutions but apply very well to the EU.[8]

Easton identified two main types of support for a political system: *affective support*, which is based on an ideological, sociological or cultural attachment; and *utilitarian support*, which is based on rational calculations of material costs and benefits. Rather than seeing these two types of support as opposing, Easton saw them as related. Affective support provides a basic reservoir of good will towards a political system. Some citizens have a high level of affective support while others have a low level. Then, utilitarian calculations determine whether this basic reservoir of support goes up and down. If a citizen perceives that she benefits from a political system, her underlying level of support will increase, while if she perceives that she loses, her underlying level of support will decrease. These utilitarian calculations can be economic, in terms of whether an individual gains or loses financially from the EU. They can also be political, in terms of whether an individual agrees or disagrees with particular EU policies.

These ideas go a long way towards explaining the changing levels of support for the EU amongst the member states.[9] For example, Dutch citizens originally had very high levels of affective support for European integration, regarding the EU project as essential for peace and security in Europe. However, the Netherlands has now overtaken Germany as the largest net contributor per capita into the EU budget, which seems rather unjust to many Dutch citizens given that they are not the richest member state in the EU. Growing perceptions that others are benefiting more than the Netherlands has consequently led to a decline in support in that country. The story for Italy is similar: an initially high level of support for European integration based on an ideological commitment to European integration rather than rational economic interest calculations, but then a decline in support as a result of growing perceptions that Italy is benefiting less from the internal market and the single currency than many other member states, particular after the 2004 EU enlargement.

From the other extreme, the contrast between the United Kingdom and Ireland is telling. When Ireland and the UK joined in 1973, the basic level of (affective) support for the EU was low in both these countries. The initial decision to join in both countries was based less on an ideological commitment to European integration than a belief that they would benefit from the common market. Since joining, however, Ireland seems to have benefited far more than the UK; with enormous investment in Ireland from mainly American business, to get a foothold in the internal market, and large financial transfers to Ireland from the EU's regional funds. As a result, public support for the EU in Ireland rose dramatically (until the early 1990s), while in the UK it has barely changed in the last thirty years from the low start in the mid 1970s.

Cost–benefit calculations also explain variations in public support at the individual level. For example, one group in society that has benefited enormously from European integration is the economic, political and social elite. European integration has provided elites with new opportunities to live and work where they choose, to travel more freely and cheaply, to interact with a greater number of people, and to make the most of their human capital (their educational levels and economic assets). Not surprisingly, while public support for the EU at the mass level has declined, Europe's economic, political and social elites remain strongly committed to the project.

The gap between the attitudes of the elites and the masses is illustrated in figure 4.4. The data here are from a special Eurobarometer survey in Spring 1996, when pollsters interviewed between 200 and 500 politicians, senior civil servants, business and trade union leaders, media owners and editors, influential academics, and leading cultural and religious

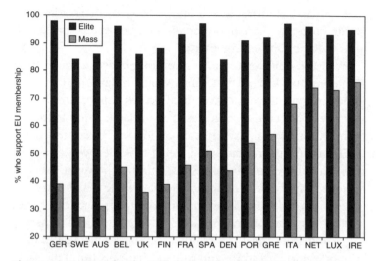

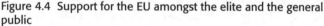

Figure 4.4 Support for the EU amongst the elite and the general
public

Source: Author's calculations from the Eurobarometer Elite Survey (Autumn
1996) and the standard Eurobarometer 46 survey (Autumn 1996). The
member states are sorted from the largest elite–mass gap, on the left, to the
smallest elite–mass gap, on the right.

figures in every member state. Whereas only 48 per cent of the
general public supported EU membership at that time, 94 per
cent of the elites supported it. The figure also shows a more
uniform set of attitudes amongst the elites than amongst the
mass publics, as indicated by the smaller variation in the elite
scores across the member states.

Cost–benefit calculations are also significant in explaining
individual-level variations in attitudes towards the EU at the
mass level. Most citizens are not able to calculate the precise
costs and benefits of the EU for them personally. However,
each citizen can build up a relatively accurate perception of
whether the EU benefits 'someone like me' from personal
experience and from information and cues from trusted

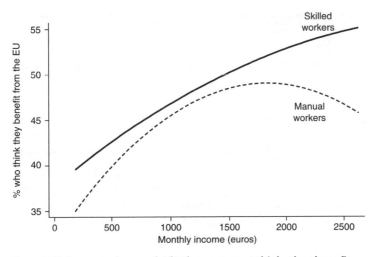

Figure 4.5 Income, class and whether someone thinks they benefit from the EU

Note: Author's calculations using the Mannheim Eurobarometer Trend File, 1970–2002. These are fitted quadratic regression lines, from the data in the 2000–2 Eurobarometer surveys.

sources, such as conversations with colleagues and friends, newspaper and TV reports, from statements by the professional associations or social groups to which they belong, or from positions taken by the political parties for whom they vote.

The different attitudes of skilled and manual workers is particularly instructive in this regard, as figure 4.5 shows. In general, skilled workers are slightly more favourable towards the EU than manual workers. Also, better paid skilled workers are more supportive of the EU than less well paid skilled workers. This reflects the fact that amongst skilled workers the level of pay is a reflection of a person's skill level, which in turn is an indicator of how much a person can potentially benefit from market liberalisation in Europe – since workers with higher skills are more able to move to better jobs or attract firms and capital to use their skills better.

In contrast, how much a manual worker is paid is not exclusively determined by the worker's skill level. Another factor determining the pay of manual workers is how well organised they are. For example, manual workers in the manufacturing sectors in Scandinavia, the Benelux, France and Germany have managed to secure comparatively high wages because they are well organised. For these workers, market liberalisation in Europe is a potential threat, as it allows capital to flee to less-well-organised and cheaper manual workers in other member states, such as the new member states in Central and Eastern Europe. As a result, the gap in the level of support for the EU between skilled workers and manual workers increases as the incomes of the two groups rises: with higher paid skilled workers benefiting *more* from the EU than less well paid skilled workers, while higher paid manual workers benefit *less* from the EU than less well paid manual workers.

However, the EU is more than simply an internal market. As discussed in the previous two chapters, EU policies cover a wide range of social and economic policies, and the policy regimes produced by the EU constrain the policy choices of national governments. So, when making utilitarian calculations about the costs and benefits of the EU, citizens consider a lot more than their personal economic situation. They also consider the likely political and policy consequences of the EU relative to their own policy preferences.

How these 'political calculations' shape attitudes towards the EU is clearly illustrated in the cases of Britain and France. Britain has a relatively liberal market economy with a less regulated labour market and a lower level of public expenditure than the EU average. France, in contrast, has a more *dirigiste* economic model, with a more regulated labour market and a higher level of public expenditure than the EU average.

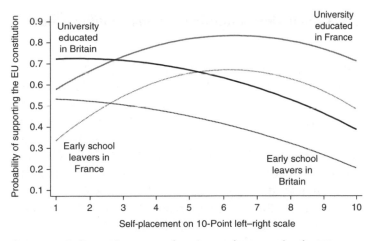

Figure 4.6 Policy preferences, education and support for the EU
Constitution in Britain and France

Note: Author's calculations from Eurobarometer 64.2 (Autumn
2005). Separate logit models of British and French support for the
constitution were estimated, with controls for a respondent's age and
knowledge of the EU.

Policies from the EU, as I discussed in the previous chapter,
tend to be quite centrist. But, because existing policies in
Britain and France were on opposite sides of the EU's political
centre, the EU has led to higher social protection and workers'
rights in Britain but lower social protection and workers' rights
in France. So, left-wing British citizens and right-wing French
citizens are the 'policy winners' from the EU, while right-wing
British citizens and left-wing French citizens are the 'policy
losers' from the EU. As figure 4.6 shows, this explains why
the right in France and the left in Britain supported the
Constitution, while the left in France and the right in Britain
opposed it, irrespective of the basic socio-economic interests of
a citizen (as measured here by a citizen's level of educational
attainment).

Conclusion: a public relations strategy is not enough

Public support for the EU is at an all-time low. This is not just because the EU has expanded to include countries whose citizens are not as ideologically committed to European integration as the citizens in some countries in Western Europe used to be. More worryingly, the citizens of most of the founding member states are less supportive of the EU and are far less willing to accept decisions of their own governments at the European level than they used to be. The reservoir of ideological support for European integration that once existed in the founding countries has gradually dried up.

Pretending that growing public opposition towards the EU will simply go away, for example if the EU economy grew faster, is completely delusional. Economic growth may mean that some people will look at the EU in a more favourable way. However, for most people, whether they support or oppose the EU is now down to narrow economic and political calculations. In this regards, what shapes French, Dutch, Italian and German citizens' attitudes towards the EU is no different from what shapes Irish, British, Swedish, Portuguese, Polish or Czech citizens' attitudes.

Put simply, citizens who perceive that they gain new economic opportunities from market integration in Europe tend to support the EU, while citizens who perceive that market integration threatens their economic interests tend to oppose the EU. Moreover, citizens who feel that EU policies (such as social and environmental regulations) are closer to their personal political views than their current national policies are likely to support the EU, while citizens who feel that EU policies are further from their personal political views than their current national policies are likely to oppose the EU.

This is a difficult environment for Europe's leaders, since a public relations campaign aimed at raising the profile of the EU amongst Europe's citizens is unlikely to succeed – as has been clearly demonstrated with the rejection of the Constitution. Explaining what the EU does and how it works is surely a good thing. However, as citizens gain more information about the EU they also understand whether or not they benefit or whether or not the EU is producing policies they like. While the EU was building the internal market, which had huge potential collective gains, more information about the EU led to more public support. However, with enlargement of the EU to new member states with significantly lower production costs and lower incomes than many of the founding member states, with economic and monetary union constraining public spending, and with the new economic reforms, more information about the EU simply means that who wins and who loses from the new policy context is increasingly transparent. Winners, such as unskilled workers in Central and Eastern Europe and higher income earners in the older member states, will continue to support the EU, while losers, such as manual workers and public sector workers in the older member states, will increasingly oppose the EU.

Furthermore, as the EU makes choices about how liberalised or regulated the internal market should be, more information about the EU will make it clearer to citizens whether they agree or disagree with EU policies. Since most existing EU policies are relatively centrist, any change means some citizens will be opposed while others will be in favour. In general, right-wing citizens will favour more liberalisation while left-wing citizens will oppose this. So, a public relations campaign will not be enough to persuade citizens that labour market reform or service sector liberalisation is a good thing.

The level of popular legitimacy of the EU is dangerously low. Making the EU more transparent and more efficient or telling citizens more about the EU is a start, but it is not enough to convince citizens that the EU is still necessary or that new policy actions by the EU are legitimate. In democratic political systems, if a citizen loses from a particular policy or suffers economic hardship, the citizen does not blame the political system as a whole, but rather blames the government of the day. In the EU, in contrast, those who lose from economic integration or from policy reforms simply blame the EU system as a whole, as they do not perceive a governing coalition at the European level who they can replace. Hence, the question of how to overcome growing opposition to the EU amongst those who feel they do not gain from the EU is inextricably linked to the question of the EU 'democratic deficit', which is the subject of the next chapter.

CHAPTER FIVE

A democratic deficit

Concerns about a 'democratic deficit' in the EU were first expressed by anti-Europeans and pro-Europeans alike in the mid 1980s. These concerns were initially voiced by politicians, policy-makers and political scientists who argued that the Single European Act had passed significant powers up to the European level without sufficient parliamentary or judicial control on these powers. In the mid 1990s, with the emergence of popular opposition to the Maastricht Treaty and the related collapse in public support for the EU, these voices became louder and concerns started to be expressed more widely, by interest groups, journalists, political parties and private citizens.

The democratic deficit was initially only a concern in member states that had a history of stable democratic institutions, such as Denmark, Sweden, France, the United Kingdom and the Netherlands. These days, these concerns are expressed across Europe: in established democracies, in the founding member states who had relatively weak democratic traditions (Germany and Italy), in the states that became democratic in the 1970s (Spain, Portugal and Greece), and in many of the new democracies in Central and Eastern Europe (particularly in Poland, the Czech Republic, Estonia and Latvia). For example, in the new member states, many citizens are reluctant to hand over their new democratic rights to the EU's 'unelected government'. Throughout Europe, people who regard the EU as undemocratic tend to be strongly opposed to the EU, irrespective of which member state they live in or their personal economic interests or political preferences.[1] So, whether or not the EU actually does have a democratic deficit, there is a growing perception that the EU is an undemocratic system and that something should be done about it.

There is no single definition of the democratic deficit in the EU. Definitions are as varied as the nationality, political views and preferred solutions of the academics and commentators who write about it. Nevertheless, it is possible to identify a limited number of 'standard claims' about the democratic deficit.[2] Most of these claims can be refuted. However, one particular claim, that there is no competition for control of political authority at the European level, is difficult to refute. This is a big problem, as competition for political power is *the* essential element of virtually all modern theories of democratic government. Even if a polity is procedurally democratic, in terms of having representative institutions and checks-and-balances on the exercise of power, it is not substantively democratic unless there is open competition for executive office and over the direction of the policy agenda. Put this way, the EU is closer to a form of enlightened despotism than a form of democratic government.[3]

Five standard claims about the EU democratic deficit

There are five standard claims about the democratic deficit in the EU. The first claim is that European integration has led to an increase in executive power and a decrease in national parliamentary control.[4] At the domestic level in Europe the central institutions of representative government are the national parliaments. National parliaments may have few formal powers of legislative amendment, but each parliament can hire and fire the cabinet, and the executive is held to account by parliamentary scrutiny of government ministers. In contrast, executive actors are dominant at the European level: national ministers in the Council and government appointees in the European Commission. This, by itself, is not a problem. However, these EU level executive actors are largely beyond the control of national parliaments. Even with the establishment of European Affairs Committees in all national parliaments, ministers when speaking and voting in the Council, national bureaucrats when making policies in working groups of the Council, and officials in the Commission when drafting or implementing legislation, are largely isolated from national parliamentary scrutiny and control. As a result, it is often claimed that European integration has meant a decrease in the power of national parliaments and an increase in the power of executives.

The second claim, which is related to the first, is that the European Parliament is too weak. In the 1980s some people argued that there was a trade-off between the powers of the European Parliament and the powers of national parliaments, where any increase in the powers of the European Parliament would mean a decrease in the powers of national parliaments. However, by the 1990s this position disappeared as scholars started to see European integration as a decline in the power of national parliaments relative to national executives. The solution, many argued, was to increase the power of the European Parliament relative to the governmental actors in the Council and Commission.[5] As discussed in chapter 3, successive reforms of the EU treaties since the mid 1980s have increased the powers of the European Parliament, exactly as many of the democratic deficit scholars had advocated. Nevertheless, a significant proportion of EU legislation is still passed under the consultation procedure, where the European Parliament does not have the power to amend or block legislation. The European Parliament does not have the same power as the

Council to amend all areas of the EU budget. And, although the European Parliament can now vote on the Commission President and the team of Commissioners, the governments are still the agenda-setters in the appointment of the Commission.

The third claim is that, despite the growing power of the European Parliament, there is not a democratic electoral contest for EU political office or over the direction of the EU policy agenda. Citizens elect their governments, who sit in the Council and nominate commissioners. Citizens also elect the European Parliament. However, neither national elections nor European Parliament elections are really 'European' contests, in that they are not about the personalities and parties at the European level or the direction of the EU policy agenda. National elections are fought on domestic rather than European issues, and political parties collude to keep the issue of Europe off the domestic agenda. European Parliament elections are also not really about EU office holders or EU policy issues, because national parties and the national media treat these elections as mid-term contests in the national electoral cycle. I discuss this in more detail below. Suffice it to say at this stage that the absence of a 'European' element in national and European elections means that citizens' preferences on issues on the EU policy agenda at best have only an indirect influence on EU policy outcomes. In comparison, if the EU were a system with a genuine electoral contest to determine who governs at the European level, the outcome of this election would have a direct influence on what EU leaders do.

The fourth claim is that the EU is simply 'too distant' from voters. The EU is too different from the domestic democratic institutions that citizens are used to. As a result, citizens cannot understand the EU, and so will never be able to assess and regard it as an accountable system of government, nor to identify with it. For example, the Commission is neither a government nor a bureaucracy, and is appointed through what appears to be an obscure procedure rather than elected directly by the votes or indirectly after a parliamentary election. The Council meanwhile is part legislature and part executive, and when acting as a legislature its deliberations and decisions are usually in secret. And, the European Parliament cannot be a properly deliberative assembly because of the multilingual nature of debates in committees and the plenary.

The fifth claim is that there is a gap between the policies that citizens want and the policies they actually get, largely as a result of the other four factors. The EU adopts policies that are not supported by a majority of citizens in many or even most member states. Governments can undertake policies at the European level that they cannot pursue at the domestic level, where they are constrained by parliaments, courts and well-organised interest groups. These policy outcomes include a neo-liberal internal market, a monetarist framework for EMU, huge subsidies to farmers, and restrictive immigration and police cooperation policies. Because EU policy outcomes are generally to the right of domestic policies in some member states, these arguments are often made by social democratic politicians and scholars.[6] A variant of this 'social democratic critique' focuses on the role of the business lobby in Brussels. Business interests and multinational firms have a greater incentive to organise at the European level than diffuse interests, such as consumer groups or trade unions. Also, because a classic representative chamber, such as the European Parliament, is not the dominant institution in EU governance, interest group politics are not counterbalanced by democratic party politics in EU policy-making. As a result, some scholars claim that EU policy outcomes are skewed more towards the interests of the owners of capital than is the case for policy compromises at the national level in Europe.[7]

Why four of these claims are largely wrong

At face value these claims seem reasonable and add up to a fairly damning critique of the democratic foundations of the EU. However, there are good reasons to challenge most of these claims, as Andrew Moravcsik, one of the biggest names in EU studies, has recently done.[8]

The first claim, that the EU has led to a shift in power from parliaments to governments, is largely incorrect because the most directly accountable politicians in Europe are national governments not national parliaments. National elections are less about the make-up of parliaments than about which parties should form the government and which party leader should be the prime minister. Also, it is a myth that national parliaments were once 'in control' of national governments and are now toothless because of European integration. In Europe's parliamentary systems, governments have always dominated parliaments. Governments have a monopoly on information and expertise in policy-making. Governments normally command a majority in their parliaments, which relegates parliaments to simply 'rubberstamping' bodies rather than genuine legislative-amendment chambers (like the US Congress). So, if national governments are the most accountable institutions in European politics, allowing them to dominate decision-making in the EU has not really eroded the authority of national parliaments.

One could go even further, and make the point that when the EU was a purely intergovernmental organisation (before the Single European Act), where each national government had the right to block a decision, there were no concerns about the democratic deficit. The problem now, though, is that the EU is a more majoritarian system, where most decisions by the governments are made by QMV and the three supranational institutions (the Commission, the European Parliament and the

Court of Justice) can shape policy outcomes beyond the original intentions of some of the governments. Moving away from the intergovernmental model was essential for the creation and regulation of the internal market and for the adoption of flanking social and environmental policies. However, majoritarian decision-making in the Council means that the EU is less directly accountable than it was when it was purely an intergovernmental organisation.

Having said that, and against the claim that the European Parliament needs to be strengthened, the most important institutional development in the last two decades has been the increased powers of the European Parliament. It is correct to claim that national governments no longer dominate outcomes because significant agenda-setting power has been delegated to the Commission and because QMV has been introduced and extended in the Council. As a result of these changes, indirect accountability via national governments in the Council is weaker than it used to be. However, successive reforms of the treaties have addressed this potential problem by radically increasing the powers of the European Parliament in exactly these areas. In almost all areas where QMV has been introduced in the Council for the adoption of legislation, the European Parliament has been granted power to amend and veto legislation. In particular, under the co-decision procedure, which is used for most legislation covering the creation and regulation of the internal market, the Council decides by QMV and legislation cannot be passed without the positive assent of the European Parliament. So, if a party in government is on the losing side of a qualified-majority vote in the Council, it has a chance of 'winning it back' in the European Parliament, as Germany has done on several occasions (such as the Takeover Directive in July 2001). In addition, the European Parliament now has veto power over the selection of the Commission and is increasingly willing to use this power against heavy lobbying from national governments, as was seen with the European Parliament's rejection of the initial line-up of the Barroso Commission in October 2004.

The third claim, that the EU is too distant and too opaque, ignores the fact that EU policy-making is now more transparent than most domestic systems of government. The paranoia inside the EU institutions about their isolation from citizens and the new internal rules in response to public and media accusations have made it much easier for interest groups, the media, national politicians and private citizens to access EU documents and information. The EU's extensive web-based document and legislative-tracking service is the 'gold standard' for many national governments and international organisations.[9] EU technocrats are now forced to listen to multiple societal interests. The European Court of Justice and national courts exercise extensive judicial review of EU actions. And, the European Parliament and national parliaments are increasingly able to scrutinise the drafting of legislation inside the Commission and the Council as well as in the implementation of EU legislation at the European and national levels.

The only area where EU decision-making could be more transparent is inside the Council. More Council documents are now publicly available, and the results of recorded votes are now published in the Council's minutes. When the Council takes executive decisions, for example on most issues in the Common Foreign and Security Policy, it makes sense that sensitive decisions between executive actors should be made 'behind closed doors'. However, when the Council is acting as a legislative body, for example as it does under the co-decision procedure, Council decision-making should be far more transparent than it currently is. Citizens should be able to see which government proposed what, which amendments to legislation passed and which failed, and who was on the winning and losing side in each vote. In short, the Council should be organised more like a normal legislature, with transparent amendment rules and public debates. Without this, citizens cannot really see what their governments are doing in their name when making EU laws.

Against the fifth claim, that EU policies are systematically biased in a right-wing direction against the policy preferences of the average voter, recall the argument in chapter 3: that because of the checks-and-balances in the EU system most policy outputs are very centrist. The institutional design of the EU means that broad coalitions are required for policies to be adopted. Unanimous agreement amongst the governments (and ratification by national parliaments or referendums) is required to delegate policies to the European level or to introduce QMV in a particular policy area. Then, under the main legislative procedure (the co-decision procedure), law can only be passed if it is supported by a majority in the Commission, QMV in the Council, and a majority in the European Parliament. Then, once adopted, EU law is subject to judicial review by national courts and the European Court of Justice. Also, no single set of private interests can dominate the EU policy process, the main parties on the centre-left and centre-right are represented in the Council and the Commission, and the full spectrum of European political opinions are represented in the European Parliament.

As a result of the centrist policy outcomes of the EU, radical free marketeers are just as frustrated with the EU as left-wing socialists. This explains why the British Conservative Party, which for a long time has been the most right-wing party on the mainstream centre-right, and the French Socialist Party, who are the most left-wing party on the mainstream centre-left, are both relatively anti-European because they are both far away from the centrist policy outcomes of the EU. In contrast, all the conservative, Christian democrat, liberal and social democratic parties between the British conservatives and

French socialists are much more pro-European than these two parties because they are closer to the average EU policies.

In sum, as Andrew Moravcsik succinctly put it:

> Constitutional checks and balances, indirect democratic control via national governments, and the increasing powers of the European Parliament are sufficient to ensure that EU policy-making is, in nearly all cases, clean, transparent, effective and politically responsive to the demands of European citizens.[10]

Four of the five standard claims about the democratic deficit are relatively easy to refute. However, the remaining claim, that there is no democratic contest for control of political authority at the European level, is harder to deny.

The missing element: a contest for EU power and policy

Most theorists of democratic government highlight two different sides of democracy: a procedural side, and a substantive side. The procedural side relates to the rules of democratic government. For a political system to be considered to be democratic it must accord to what Abraham Lincoln famously described as 'government by the people, for the people'. In modern representative democracy, government by the people means government by the elected representatives of the people. Other minimal procedural requirements are free and fair elections, universal suffrage, rights of citizens to run for political office, and freedom of speech, the press and association.[11]

The substantive side of democracy, in contrast, relates to the content of the political process. It is not enough to have representative institutions and free and fair elections if these elections are uncontested or do not change political outcomes. Joseph Schumpeter was one of the first to realise this, when he proposed that the real essence of modern democracy – against the classical view based mainly on procedural requirements – was a battle between political elites for control of political authority.[12] In a similar vein, as Elmer Schattschneider put it, democracy is 'a competitive political system in which competing leaders and organizations define the alternatives of public policy in such a way that the public can participate in the decision-making process'.[13] In practical terms this means a contest over two things: executive office, and the direction of the policy agenda. Contests for control of the executive and over the policy agenda enable citizens to identify the winners (who form the government) and the losers (who become part of the opposition).[14]

The EU meets all the procedural requirements to be considered a democratic polity. A basic requirement of the treaties is that the member states must be representative democracies, have free and fair elections, and promote freedom of expression and association. Citizens are represented in the EU's institutions: directly in the European Parliament, and indirectly in the Council and Commission. Citizens are free to stand in European Parliament elections, and these elections are free and fair.

However, the EU falls well short of the substantive requirements, since there is no electoral contest for political leadership at the European level or over the direction of the EU policy agenda. Starting with the Commission, the powers of the Commission President, in terms of the Commission's monopoly of legislative initiative and the ability of the Commission President to assign portfolios in the Commission, are similar to those of prime ministers in domestic cabinet governments. Formally, the European Commission is indirectly elected, by the governments and the European Parliament. In practice, however, the Commission President is appointed through top-secret negotiations and horse-trading between the EU heads of government. As a result, the election of the Commission President is closer to the election of a pope – who emerges from a secret conclave of cardinals – than to an open and competitive battle between politicians with rival policy agendas for their term in office.

The process of electing national governments is not much better where politics at the European level is concerned. For sure, national general elections are the most competitive and democratic processes in European politics. The problem, though, is that these elections are about national executive office and national policy issues rather than European executive office and European level policy issues. For example, when competing in national elections, political parties do not say who they will support for Commission President. And, despite the fact that a large part of national government business is devoted to scrutinising and passing EU legislation, less than 2 per cent of national parties' election manifestos are dedicated to EU policy issues.[15] This is of course understandable. It is rational for voters, parties and the media to focus on national-level issues in national elections, because what is at stake at the European level in these elections is smaller than what is at stake at the national level, in terms of who gets to control national policy-making and public spending. However, this means that national government elections cannot ever be a substitute for a genuine contest for political authority at the European level.

Referendums on EU issues, such as joining the EU or the single currency or on a new EU treaty, do better than national elections in terms of allowing voters to express their preferences about the EU.[16] National politics, such as the popularity of the government at the time of a referendum, have some influence on how citizens vote in EU referendums. However, in most cases, referendums promote public debates about the EU in the member states involved and allow citizens to make

a choice about a particular issue on the EU agenda. The problem with referendums, however, is that they only allow
voters to express their views about isolated and mainly constitutional issues and not on who forms the executive at the
European level or about the direction of the EU policy agenda.
This means that referendums are not very effective at
connecting citizens' views on EU-level issues and EU policy
outputs.

But, what about European Parliament elections? Unlike
national elections and EU referendums, these contests involve
the election of an institution which can influence who holds
EU executive office, via the European Parliament's role in the
election of the Commission, and the direction of the EU policy
agenda, via the European Parliament's legislative powers. This
was the main idea behind the introduction of these elections.
As Walter Hallstein, who was President of the Commission
between 1958 and 1967, put it:

> [European Parliament elections] would force those entitled to
> vote to look at and examine the questions and the various
> options on which the European Parliament would have to
> decide in the months and years ahead. It would give candi-
> dates who emerged victorious from such a campaign a truly
> European mandate from their electors; and it would encour-
> age the emergence of truly European political parties.[17]

Sadly, after six rounds of European Parliament elections, the
reality is quite different.

The problem is that European Parliament elections actually
have very little to do with 'Europe'! These elections are not
about rival candidates for the Commission President, or even
about which political party should be the largest group in the
European Parliament, or even about whether a particular MEP
has done a good or bad job in the European Parliament.
Instead, voters, the media and national parties treat European
Parliament elections as just another set of domestic elections,

where the dominant issue is how well national governments have performed.

European Parliament elections are in fact 'second-order national elections'. This conception was first put forward by Karlheinz Reif and Hermann Schmitt after studying the results of the first European Parliament elections in 1979,[18] and is still true after the most recent elections in June 2004.[19] Basically, national government elections are the primary contests throughout Europe. Parties, voters and the media consequently treat all other elections – European Parliament elections, regional and local elections, second chamber elections, and elections to choose a ceremonial head of state – as secondary contests, as part of the on-going first-order election process.

This has two effects. First, because second-order elections are less important, there is less incentive for people to vote in these elections. So, about 20 per cent fewer people vote in European Parliament elections than in national elections, and turnout in the 2004 European Parliament elections fell to below 50 per cent of eligible voters for the first time.

Second, because European Parliament elections are really about the performance of national governments but do not lead to the formation of a new national government, the people who do vote in these elections vote differently than if a national election were held at the same time. On the one hand, voters use European Parliament elections to express their views about particular policy issues they care about, such as the environment or immigration, rather than to vote for one of the larger parties that is likely to form a government. This effect means that large parties, whether in government or opposition, lose votes in European Parliament elections to smaller parties. On the other hand, voters use European Parliament elections to express their dissatisfaction with the current policies or the leaders of a party or parties in government. This

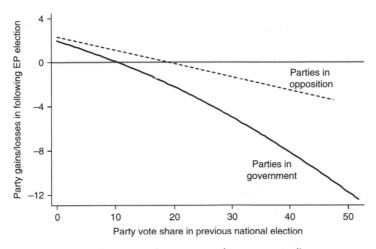

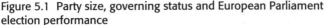

Figure 5.1 Party size, governing status and European Parliament
election performance

Note: Author's calculations from data used in Hix and Marsh (2007).
These functions are simple bivariate quadratic regression models of the
relationship between a party's vote share in the previous general election and
whether the party gained or lost votes in an EP election, pooled for all EP
elections between 1979 and 2004 in all member states, and estimated
separately for parties in government and parties in opposition at the time
of the EP election.

effect means that governing parties lose votes in European
Parliament elections to opposition parties.

Figure 5.1 consequently shows how parties performed in
European Parliament elections relative to the previous
national election, for all political parties in all the member
states in all six sets of European Parliament elections between
1979 and 2004. The two separate second-order effects are
clearly visible: (1) larger parties do much worse than smaller
parties in these contests (relative to their national electoral performance), regardless of whether a party is in government
or opposition; and (2) governing parties get fewer votes in
European Parliament elections than opposition parties.

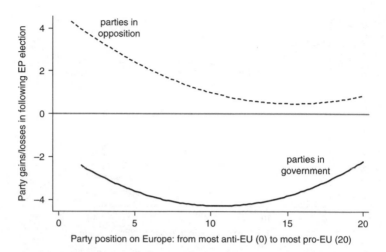

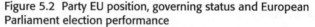

Party position on Europe: from most anti-EU (0) to most pro-EU (20)

Figure 5.2 Party EU position, governing status and European
Parliament election performance

Note: Author's calculations from data used in Hix and Marsh (2007).
Party positions on Europe are measured from surveys of political
scientists, who were asked to locate parties on a 20-point anti-/pro-EU
scale. The two functions are simple bivariate quadratic regression models
of the relationship between a party's position on Europe and whether the
party gained or lost votes in an EP election, pooled for all EP elections
between 1979 and 2004 in all member states, and estimated separately
for parties in government and parties in opposition at the time of the
EP election.

This may seem surprising to some people, since the media
often report that European Parliament elections are about EU
issues, particularly as anti-European parties appear to do well
in these elections. For example, following the 2004 elections,
Raphael Minder and George Parker wrote in *The Financial
Times* that: 'Europe was in handwringing mode yesterday as
the political elite surveyed the wreckage of Sunday's European
election results: a scene of voter apathy, government-bashing
and anti-European Union sentiment.'[20] Figure 5.2 investigates
whether 'Europe' plays a role, by showing the performance of

parties in all the European Parliament elections relative to the previous national election, according to their policy positions towards the EU (whether they are pro- or anti-European) and their governing status. The results show that amongst governing parties, strongly pro- and strongly anti-European parties lose slightly fewer votes in European Parliament elections than governing parties with more moderate views on Europe. Also, amongst opposition parties, anti-European parties do better than pro-European parties.

However, the main effect in figure 5.2 is the gap between opposition and governing parties, which has nothing to do with whether these parties are pro- or anti-European. And, the effect of parties' EU policy positions is actually indistinguishable from the non-Europe related effects, because almost all anti-European parties are actually small opposition parties. We know, however, that other small parties – such as anti-immigrant parties, green parties, extreme left parties and regionalist parties – do well in European Parliament elections, regardless of their attitudes towards Europe. This consequently suggests that the main reason that anti-European parties do well in European Parliament elections is that they are small opposition parties, and so provide a home for voters who would like to protest against the national governments or the larger opposition parties.

An increasing number of citizens are aware of the importance of the European Parliament and trust the European Parliament more than the other EU institutions. For example, in the Eurobarometer survey in Autumn 2005, 52 per cent of citizens said that they trusted the European Parliament to protect their interests, whereas only 48 per cent said that they trusted the Commission. Despite this, the evidence overwhelmingly suggests that voters use European Parliament elections to influence government and policies at the national level rather than the European level.

This is not irrational behaviour by voters. The European Parliament is elected by a system of proportional representation, which means that the location of the median member of the European Parliament is only ever likely to shift slightly to the left or slightly to the right as a result of European Parliament elections. Also, despite the growing powers of the European Parliament, the checks-and-balances in the EU legislative process mean that any change in the make-up of the European Parliament resulting from European Parliament elections does not lead directly to a change in EU policies. And, European Parliament elections do not really change the balance of power inside the European Parliament because agenda-setting powers in the chamber (in terms of the committee chairs and the legislative rapporteurships) are allocated proportionally rather than through a winner-takes-all system (as in most national parliaments in Europe, or in the US Congress).

As a result of all these factors, the potential European-level impact of European Parliament elections is far less important for most voters than the potential national level impact, in terms of whether these contests lead to changes in the policies of the current national government or influence the outcome of the next national general election. So, in European Parliament elections, what is at stake at the national level is much greater for most voters than what is at stake at the European level.

In sum, in the way the EU currently works, there is no arena for competition over political authority in the EU. There is an extremely weak connection between voters' choices in national and European Parliament elections and the policy outcomes at the European level. National elections are about national executive figures and the national policy agenda, and so too are European Parliament elections. As a result, even if the EU could be considered a democratic system in a procedural sense it is a long way from being considered a democratic system in a substantive sense.

Conclusion: the EU is a form of enlightened despotism not a democracy

Against the overblown claims of some of the critics of the EU, the EU has all the procedural elements of democracy, in terms of representative institutions, free and fair elections, and checks-and-balances on the exercise of power.[21] These procedural elements guarantee that most EU policy outcomes are close to the policy preferences of some hypothetical European-wide average citizen.[22]

However, ensuring that policies are close to some notional average European citizen is not enough for the EU to be considered to be a democratic system. What is missing is the substantive content of democracy: a battle for control of political power and the policy agenda at the European level, between rival groups of leaders with rival policy platforms, where the winners and losers of this battle are clearly identifiable, and where the winners have a reasonable chance of losing next time round and the losers have a reasonable chance of winning. Without such a democratic contest we simply do not know, *a priori*, whether the policies of the EU really are the choices of European citizens.

In fact, without a competition for political power, the EU is closer to a form of enlightened despotism than a genuine democracy. Enlightened despotism is a form of government which emerged in Europe in the eighteenth century, where monarchs agreed to consult representative bodies (the early parliaments), and were limited by constitutional rules and judicial bodies, and so generally enacted policies that promoted the interests of their citizens. This was much better than previous forms of authoritarian government, where the ruling classes used their powers to promote their private economic and political interests against the general interests of the citizens. But, enlightened despotism is quite different from what came after it: genuinely democratic government, with competitive elections to determine who would form the government. Without a democratic contest, where citizens participate actively in the battle for political office and the policy agenda, the EU cannot be a democratic system of government.

Recognising a democratic deficit in the EU, most commentators then draw one of two conclusions: a Eurosceptic conclusion, that because the EU is not democratic, significant powers should be handed back to national governments; or a Eurofederalist conclusions, that the EU will only be democratic if it is transformed into a full-blown federal state.

I do not fall into either of these traps. Against a Eurosceptic position, I recognise that the EU is needed more than ever, as I explained in chapter 2. Against the Eurofederalist position, European citizens are probably not ready for the EU to be transformed into a federation. Turning the EU into a United States of Europe would have profound and uncertain political consequences and as a result is rejected by most European citizens. Also, European parties and voters are probably not ready for European-scale direct democracy, as the failure of European Parliament elections to create a contest for European power has vividly demonstrated.

Nevertheless, concerns about the democratic deficit will not go away, and need to be addressed. The best way to do this, I contend, is to inject more political competition into EU political processes, to gradually develop what I call 'limited democratic politics'. This will not make the EU fully democratic, but it may be the best we can hope for at this stage of the EU's development, as it would allow the EU to work in a more open and democratic way than it currently does, and may in time generate demands from citizens for a more directly democratic contest for power at the European level.

PART II

The Cure

CHAPTER SIX

The case for 'limited democratic politics' in the EU

For a long time, 'politics', meaning open contests over political authority and the direction of the policy agenda, has been absent from the EU. This was justifiable while the main issue on the EU agenda was how to construct the basic political and economic architecture of a continental-scale polity. This required unanimous agreement amongst all the member states and all the main political traditions in Europe, to ensure that all countries and mainstream political groups benefited in some way from the basic institutional and policy set-up of the EU. But, some groups have lost from European integration and now that the policy agenda of the EU has shifted from polity-building to what economic and social policies should be pursued in the new European-scale polity, political conflict is beginning to emerge as the winners and losers from EU policies take opposing sides in the debates.

Open politicisation of the EU policy process will be feared by Europe's elites. Government ministers and national party leaders will not want to reveal publicly that they lose any key battle. They should resist this temptation, and we, the citizens, should demand that political contests, and the winners and losers of these contests, are out in the open.

Many people are turned off by politics, as it seems nasty, parochial and divisive. However, there are good reasons why political competition is central to the democratic process. A contest for control of political authority and over the direction of the policy agenda forces elites to reveal their policy preferences to

the public and encourages leaders to engage in policy innovation and joined-up thinking across a range of policy issues. It
also allows citizens to identify the winners and losers of policy
outcomes, to gauge whether the holders of public office have
delivered on their electoral promises, to choose to support rival
leaders in the next stage of the on-going competition, and to
hence hold leaders to account.

From efficient to redistributive outcomes: why more conflict in the EU is inevitable

Jean Monnet and the other founding fathers of European integration were convinced that national rivalries and ideological
conflicts were the root causes of war and economic destruction
in the twentieth century. Their solution was a system of government at the European level that would prevent such conflicts. Their design ensured that EU policy-making would be
dominated by technocrats in independent institutions, rather
than by an elected government or parliament. They also
designed EU decision-making rules that would guarantee
'consensus' amongst all the major players, so that no country
or major social group could be on the losing side of policy outcomes from European integration.

To understand why it was reasonable to isolate the EU from
democratic politics in the initial polity-building period it is necessary to understand the difference between what political scientists call 'efficient' and 'redistributive' policies. This is
illustrated in Figure 6.1. Imagine that Europe is divided into
two groups of citizens, A and B, and that the current policy of
the EU, X, produces benefits of AX and BX for the two groups.
The EU considers two possible policy changes: Y and Z. A
move to policy Y would have a redistributive effect: making
group A better off, by $AY-AX$, but group B worse off, by $BY-
BX$. In fact, any policy change along the line that goes through

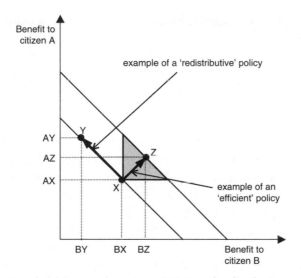

Figure 6.1 **The difference between efficient and redistributive policies**

X and Y would mean a direct redistribution of benefits from one social group to the other. In contrast, a move to policy Z would benefit both groups of citizens, by $AZ-AX$ and $BZ-BX$, respectively. In fact, any policy change from X to somewhere in the shaded area would make one group better off without making the other worse off. A policy move into this area, where everyone is better off than under the existing policy, is known as a pareto-efficient outcome, after the Italian sociologist Vilfredo Pareto.

Producing these types of 'efficient' policy outcomes is the traditional aim of social and economic regulation. In neoclassical economic theory free markets are naturally paretoefficient, but in the real world there are numerous 'market failures'. Regulation is the main instrument governments use to correct these failures. For example, technical standards and consumer protection standards enable consumers to gain information about the quality of products that would otherwise not be publicly available. Environmental standards reduce the adverse effects (negative externalities) of market transactions on individuals not participating in the transactions. And, competition policies, such as state aid rules, anti-cartel provisions and merger controls, prevent monopolies, price collusion and other market distortions.

If economic policies are made through traditional democratic institutions, such as parliaments or governments, these policies will tend to be redistributive rather than efficient. This is because parliaments and governments are controlled by particular political majorities, who will pursue policies that benefit their own supporters rather than everyone in society. Democratic government consequently tends to lead to the redistribution of resources from the losing minority to the winning majority. For example, where expenditure policies are concerned, governments on the left usually increase taxes on the wealthiest members of society and increase public spending on social benefits, whereas governments on the right tend to reduce taxes and cut benefits. If democratic majorities are allowed to govern regulatory policies, similar redistributive outcomes would result: for example, left-wing politicians would use regulation to increase the rights of workers and protect the environment, imposing costs on business, and right-wing politicians would do the opposite.

As a result, a central argument in the theory of market regulation is that if regulatory policies are meant only to correct market failures, with pareto-efficient rather than redistributive outcomes, these policies should be made by 'non-majoritarian', or independent, institutions. This is similar to the logic behind independent central banks, as a way of achieving monetary policies in the long-term interests of society as a whole. The logic of independent regulators is also similar to the normative justification for making courts independent from political control, as independent courts are more likely to protect everyone's civil and economic rights than elected political majorities, who have an incentive to promote the rights and interests of their own supporters.

If European integration was meant to lead to policy outcomes that benefited all European citizens, then it was important to isolate the EU institutions from traditional democratic politics, at least in the initial polity-building and market-creating period.[1] Because the Commission was independent from direct political control, either by the governments or from the majority in the European Parliament, the Commission was able to develop and propose social, economic and environmental standards that were in the interests of all of Europe, rather than in the interests of a particular member state or political majority. If 'normal democratic politics' had set the basic framework for the internal market, instead of EU policies promoting the European-wide interest the result would have been policies in the interests of a particular political majority. For example, rather than an internal market programme that balanced deregulation of national markets with common environmental and social standards, the EU would have had either an overtly neo-liberal project, with few social and environmental standards, or an overtly social democratic project, with high costs for business and consumers. In either of these situations, there would have been widespread opposition to the internal market programme from the supporters of the losing side. Some scholars of the EU consequently argue that a more politicised EU during this period would have undermined rather than reinforced the legitimacy of the project.[2]

However, it is not clear that European integration has always promoted the interests of all citizens in Europe and not created any losers. In reality, EU policy outcomes can be placed on a continuum, where purely pareto-efficient/public interest policies are at one end of the continuum and purely redistributive policies are at the other end. Certain technical decisions, such as EU consumer product standards and safety protection, are at the pareto-efficient extreme of this continuum. In these areas there are a limited number of correct outcomes, and the distribution of benefits and burdens is largely settled in the process of deciding on the legal and technical standards. As a result, there is a strong case for technical standards agencies, such as food safety agencies, to be isolated from political interference.

Next on an efficient-redistributive continuum are the bulk of policies relating to the construction and reregulation of the internal market. A larger market and harmonised national regulatory standards to secure market integration certainly have pareto-improving elements. Most internal market, environmental and social regulations aim to make the European-wide market work more efficiently, and so generate wealth and jobs. These policies also aim to correct certain market failures, such as environmental pollution, collectively disadvantageous practices of trade barriers and state aid, or information asymmetries in employment contracts.

However, many EU social, economic and environmental regulations have significant indirect redistributive consequences, as some groups in society clearly benefit from these policies more than others. For example, private producers for domestic markets (particularly small-scale manufacturers) are losers from the liberalisation of trade in the internal market as they now have to compete with cheaper imports from other EU member states.[3] Similarly, businesses usually have to bear the costs of environmental standards relating to the production of goods, such as factory emissions standards. This is particularly the case when similar standards are not applied by producers outside the EU, which makes it difficult for businesses located inside the EU to share the costs of these production standards with consumers. On the other hand, EU labour market regulations, such as rules on gender equality and part-time and temporary workers, significantly benefit particular employees and raise the costs for some businesses.[4]

At the predominantly redistributive extreme, meanwhile, are the various EU spending policies. These policies mainly transfer resources from taxpayers across the EU to farmers (under the Common Agricultural Policy) and economically deprived regions (under the structural and regional policies). The major spending programmes of the EU have been specifically agreed in intergovernmental bargains to compensate member states who feel that they will not benefit as much as other states from major steps in the polity-building process. As a result, rather than aiming to produce redistributive outcomes, EU spending programmes aim to facilitate a basic institutional and policy design that benefits all the member states more or less equally, and so is pareto-efficient overall. For example, in the Treaty of Rome, the Common Agricultural Policy was the price demanded by France for supporting the common market, which France expected would predominantly benefit Germany, as the largest net exporter. Similarly, in the late 1980s, the doubling of regional spending was the price demanded by Italy, Spain, Portugal, Greece and Ireland for supporting the single market programme, which they expected would mainly benefit the core exporting economies of the EU. The regional spending programmes also aim to enable the poorer periphery states in Europe to invest in infrastructure programmes and so compete on a level playing field in the internal market with the more developed member states.

So, it was reasonable to isolate the EU from democratic politics during the polity-building and market-creating stage, to ensure that the basic political and economic architecture was in the interest of virtually all European citizens. Because of their market-creating and market-correcting aims, many regulatory policies of the EU are purely pareto-efficient. Also, even the most explicitly redistributive policies, via the transfer of resources through the EU budget, were mainly designed to promote an overall pareto-efficient architecture, by compensating the member states and regions who potentially lost from the creation of a European-wide market.

Nevertheless, many of the social, economic and environmental regulations of the EU have created indirect winners and losers. Isolating these policies from open democratic politics means that the losers from these policies are unlikely to accept the outcomes of EU decisions. Not surprisingly, small businesses across Europe, who mainly suffer the costs of EU labour market and environmental standards in the production process, increasingly complain about the costs of 'Brussels red tape'. Likewise, industrial workers in some of the older member states in Western Europe, who feel competitive pressures from lower cost workers in some of the new member states, do not perceive that all workers benefit equally from the creation of a continental-scale internal market.

Above all, now that the EU has moved beyond polity-building and market-creating to deciding what social and economic policies should be pursued in the internal market, and particularly how the European economy should be reformed, most new policies of the EU will have more clearly redistributive consequences. Unlike the period of creating the internal market in the late 1980s and early 1990s, many questions now facing the EU are explicitly political, where citizens, interest groups, political parties and governments find themselves on different sides of the policy debates. For example, should the internal market be more liberal or more regulated? Should governments be able to protect their domestic service providers from market entrants from other member states? Should incumbent workers be protected in labour markets or should firms be allowed to hire and fire employees more easily? Should the costs of reducing carbon emissions be borne by producers or consumers? Should the macro-economic and monetary policy framework of economic and monetary union be more orthodox or more Keynesian? Should there be complete free movement of workers from the new EU member states? Should the EU have a more liberal or a more restricted immigration policy? And so on. Whereas the creation of the internal market and the adoption of market-correction regulations as part of the internal market pro-gramme probably benefited most social groups in one way or another, the policy choices that the EU is now facing will almost certainly lead to clearly identifiable winners or losers, at least in the short term.

One example of how the new EU policy agenda is explicitly 'political' is the debate about labour market reform. Realising that labour market reform is a highly salient issue, with poten-tially explosive political conflicts resulting, the EU govern-ments first tried to tackle this issue outside the formal legal framework of the EU. In March 2000, the European Council adopted the so-called Lisbon Agenda, which aimed to make the EU 'the most competitive and dynamic knowledge-based econ-omy in the world'. The Lisbon Agenda set some broad targets for action in a variety of areas, including labour market reform, and established a set of procedures for monitoring whether the governments had met these targets. In contrast to the standard EU legislative procedures, the Lisbon Agenda aimed to achieve reform through informal consultation between governments and the recognition of best practices. For example, member states have been asked to exchange information about how they regulate labour markets for small firms in the service sector – who are generating most of the new jobs in the modern economy.

However, the Lisbon Agenda has largely failed. Without formal legislation and the threat of enforcement by the Commission and the European Court of Justice there have been few incentives for governments to introduce reforms which would have significant redistributional consequences for certain categories of workers, particularly in the short term. This is not because the EU is not able to pass legislation that would gradually reform labour markets. For example, under the treaty provisions on working conditions, the EU could harmonise hiring-and-firing rules for small- and medium-sized companies. This would be a radical step which would single-handedly force all the member states to deregulate their labour markets in precisely the way they have promised to do in the Lisbon process. The Commission has not initiated such a piece of legislation, and the member states have not asked the Commission to do so, because the political elites recognise that they do not have a mandate to propose such a controversial piece of legislation which would inevitably have clear redistributional consequences. This type of economic reform is simply too 'political' for the EU to handle. The result has been procrastination and paralysis.

Why political competition is a good thing

So, growing political conflict at the European level is inescapable as the EU begins to face up to the challenges ahead. Political competition in the EU is also highly desirable for at least six inter-related reasons.

First, political competition promotes *policy innovation and joined-up policy-making*. Where do new policy ideas come from? Some politicians are naturally gifted, and can come up with brilliant new policy ideas. In general, though, political leaders are no better at innovation than the rest of us, and in fact have strong incentives not to try anything new, since new ideas might alienate traditional supporters. What forces politicians to 'think outside the box', though, is the discipline of competition and contest in the policy process. In the spotlight of media scrutiny, under pressure to perform, and with the potential of competing leaders offering rival agendas, politicians are much more innovative. Political contestation also forces politicians to explain their ideas clearly and to justify how their ideas are consistent with their other policy positions. So, if it is innovative thinking that Europe needs, political contestation is more likely to promote this than isolating EU bureaucrats, government ministers and MEPs from politics.

Related to this, political competition promotes joined-up policy-making, by forcing politicians to connect the likely effects of policy in one area to policy in other areas. Without political debate there are few incentives for politicians to coordinate their positions across issues. The result is that solutions in each separate policy area can become dangerously isolated. For example, labour market liberalisation makes sense when looking only at labour markets and restrictive monetary policies makes sense when looking only at monetary policies. However, in combination these two policies can be dangerous, as the short-term consequence of labour market reform is an increase in the number of unemployed, who are then unlikely to find new jobs if the economy is not growing fast enough. Not surprisingly, when Margaret Thatcher liberalised labour markets and 'took on' the trade unions in Britain in the 1980s, she deliberately ran an expansionary monetary policy as she knew that it would be easier to reform labour markets if the British economy was booming.

This type of joined-up policy-making will not emerge in Brussels until there is a battle for control of the policy agenda, where a coherent package of policies would need to be put together to win the political debate. For example, through an open battle of ideas a trade-off between monetary policy and labour market reform may have a chance of being established, whereby finance ministers put pressure on the European Central Bank to pursue a slightly more relaxed interest rate policy in return for the EU adopting legislation that would liberalise labour markets for small and medium-sized businesses. Similarly, on the issue of liberalisation of the service sector and labour markets, a coherent policy package could include a set of flanking policies to increase investment in education and training, which would alleviate the potential short-term effects of the resulting market restructuring for certain groups of workers.

Second, political competition promotes *the formation of cross-institutional coalitions*, which would help overcome policy gridlock in the EU and allow for the sort of joined-up policy thinking just discussed. There are multiple checks-and-balances in the EU system. For example, under the co-decision procedure legislation needs to be supported by the Commission, QMV in the Council and a majority of MEPs. As discussed in chapter 3, these multiple thresholds are not a problem when policies are adopted for the first time, as large majorities in the Commission, the Council and the European Parliament usually prefer a range of potential policies to no common policies – as was the case in the creation of the internal market. However, once an EU policy has already been adopted or if a piece of legislation involves reforming an existing set of national or European policies, the result is gridlock. This is because only a few actors are needed to prevent an overwhelming majority from undertaking policy reform. For example, under the co-decision procedure, policy change can be blocked by either a majority of commissioners, or a blocking minority of member states in the Council, or one of the main political groups in the European Parliament. This is the case with existing EU policies, such as the Common Agricultural Policy, as well as new policies that reform existing national rules, such as economic reform.

With more open political battles in the EU legislative process, both within and between the EU institutions, policy gridlock in the EU is more likely to be overcome. Political debate and competition will foster the creation of issue-specific alliances across the three EU institutions. For example, on the issue of service sector reform, a pro-reform coalition of liberals, conservatives and reformist social democrats could coordinate their positions in the Commission, the Council and the European Parliament. On the other side, there could be an anti-reform coalition of traditional socialists, greens and radical left politicians. Once these battles are out in the open, where the public can see which political leaders stand for what position and belong to which political coalition, there will be costs to breaking away from agreed positions. The result would be significantly greater policy coordination across the EU institutions, and a greater chance that gridlock would be overcome.

Organisations of national parties at the European level – such as the European People's Party, the Party of European Socialists, and the European Liberal, Democrat and Reform Party – already bring together national party leaders, the leaders of the party groups in the European Parliament, and the European commissioners from these parties. However, these are rather loose umbrella organisations with few incentives to coordinate genuine political action across the EU institutions. Without open political contestation, there are no sanctions if a national party leader signs a particular transnational party agreement, such as a statement from a party leaders' summit, and then reneges on the deal. But, with more open competition, the costs of reneging on an agreement would be higher. This would either significantly strengthen these nascent transnational party organisations or would force the realignment of these organisations and the establishment of new European-wide political forces.

Third, political competition provides *incentives for the media to cover what goes on in Brussels*. There is very little coverage of EU politics in the national television and print media. This is partly because media markets have changed in the last decade or so. In the past, public news editors – for example of the main nightly TV news programmes – were free to report the news items they felt were most important. Today, these editors are competing in a more open and competitive market, and so are primarily interested in how many units they can 'shift' relative to their competitors. This forces editors to cover political events not because they are important in and of themselves but rather because they are 'infotainment' for their viewers or readers. We tune in each day or week to hear the latest comings and goings in our favourite political 'soap opera'. And our favourite soap opera, in which newspaper and TV news editors have invested so much time and resources developing, is in national capitals rather than in Brussels. Hence, there are few incentives for editors of TV news programmes or newspapers to give up their precious time or space to cover EU politics, unless what goes on in the EU can be sold to their viewers or readers as part of national politics.

This may seem rather trivial. On the contrary, we, as citizens, are heavily reliant on editors of TV and print news for information about politics. We also pay far more attention to political events and are far more engaged with public debates if we have information about the personalities in the debates and the positions they stand for. So, we will not be able to understand or engage with politics at the European level until the media, which is still mainly at the national level, provides greater coverage of the personalities and positions of the key actors in Brussels: such as the key commissioners and the leaders of the parties in the European Parliament in addition to the leading prime ministers, foreign ministers and finance ministers in the various policy debates. But, until there is genuine political drama and intrigue in Brussels, TV and newspaper editors will have no incentive to cover EU politics.

Fourth, political deliberation *enables people to form opinions about policies*. Citizens' views on most policy questions are only partially formed. This is because most citizens have limited information about the likely consequences of policy change, and so are uncertain about how a particular policy proposal will affect their interests. This is particularly true of highly complex socio-economic issues, such as liberalisation of services or the deregulation of labour markets or the liberalisation of the free movement of persons. Without open political debate, citizens' views are easily manipulated by political entrepreneurs, such as newspaper editors, leaders of minority parties, or activists in single-issue lobby groups. If there is more open debate between the main political leaders, the protagonists are forced to set out their positions and confront their opponents in the media or outside mainstream politics. The result would be a process of policy learning, whereby citizens' original opposition to a particular policy proposal can evolve into qualified support as they understand the costs, benefits and trade-offs involved in the adoption of new policies.

One example of how political debate can lead to changes in citizens' opinions is the issue of labour market reform in Germany. In the late 1990s there was widespread opposition in Germany to the liberalisation of labour markets. Following a period of intense public debates and battles between the main political parties, both inside and outside the Bundestag, a majority of voters came around to accepting that reform was necessary and so supported reformist-oriented parties and candidates in the Bundestag elections in 2005. In the absence of any debate, the positions of the voters would still have been as they were ten years before, and the German social democrats would have had no incentive to gradually change their position on this crucial issue.

Now imagine the situation in the EU with the Services Directive. Currently there is widespread opposition to the liberalisation of the service sector in Europe, particularly in several of the 'old 15' member states. Citizens' views on this issue are soft and easily manipulated by vested interests, such as protected public sector workers and nationalistic newspapers. For example, the French media campaign against allowing 'Polish plumbers' access to the French market contradicts economic evidence which suggests that plumbing is one of the services where there is a big gap between the demand for and supply of services in the French economy. If there was a more open political debate on this issue, citizens would learn that service sector liberalisation may have short-term costs but would most likely have long-term benefits. They would also learn that the Services Directive as reformed by the European Parliament was not in fact as radical as some of the opponents claim. The result would have been a much more measured debate and a gradual change in the views of citizens on the question of service sector reform and a much lower level of public opposition to a key piece of internal market legislation.

Fifth, political competition produces *a mandate for policy change*. A mandate involves the public recognition of the winners of a political contest. On the one hand, the politician or political coalition that emerges victorious from a contest is recognised by the public as having the right to try their policy agenda. On the other hand, the politicians and their supporters on the losing side accept that they have lost, for the time being, and so are willing to allow the other side to govern. This is crucial for what political scientists call 'losers' consent': where the losers of a political contest peacefully accept the outcome rather than engaging in obstruction, protest or even violence.[5] Without a mandate, the losers of a contest or from a particular set of policies have an incentive to challenge the outcome. But, if a mandate does emerge, any challenge by the losers is deemed illegitimate and will cost them popular support.

An example of the lack of a mandate is the weakness of the Barroso Commission. Barroso was in effect 'elected' by a qualified majority in the European Council against the wishes of the

French and German governments, who had originally backed Guy Verhofstadt for the post. Once elected, Barroso realised that there were centre-right majorities in the Commission, the Council and the European Parliament. He consequently thought that the opportunity existed to undertake a set of liberal reforms. However, in the process of selecting Barroso, rival candidates had not presented their policy ideas (or manifestos) to the public, and prime ministers and party leaders in national parliaments and the European Parliament had not clearly announced their support for one candidate or another. Hence, when Barroso emerged from the 'smoke-filled rooms' of the European Council to propose a radical set of policy reforms, the losers in the election process (particularly Jacques Chirac) did not accept this reform agenda as legitimate and promised to derail the whole EU policy process unless Barroso compromised on his proposals. Had there been an open debate with Barroso emerging as the winner, he would have been able to claim a mandate and the losers would have been much less able to challenge his authority.

Finally, and perhaps most profoundly, democratic politics leads to *the formation of new political identities*. A democratic identity, or *demos* as it is known in Greek, exists where citizens of all political persuasions accept the will of a political majority. Some commentators on the EU assume that democratic politics in the EU is impossible because the EU does not already have a *demos*. For example, to make this point as starkly as possible, Joseph Weiler posits that we should imagine a hypothetical *Anschluss* between Germany and Denmark and then ask ourselves whether Danish citizens would accept the will of a majority in a new German–Danish parliament.[6] Danes, of course, would not accept such a union as legitimate because the majority would be perceived as a 'German majority' and could reasonably expect that the Danes would be the permanent minority. So, he would argue, a union between nation-states cannot be democratic.

However, most political scientists see the relationship between democracy and democratic identity the other way round. Rather than assuming that a common democratic identity is a prerequisite for democracy, a democratic identity usually does not emerge until there is genuine democratic politics. This is the experience at the national level in Europe, where the replacement of local identities by national identities took place through the process of mass electoral politics and open political contests for control of political authority and the levers of government.[7] This is also the experience in the United States. V.O. Key, the famous scholar of American public opinion, explains that a United States 'public opinion' did not replace separate state public opinions until there was a vigorous nationwide political debate in the 1930s over the new spending programmes of the US federal government.[8]

One of the key factors explaining the emergence of a democratic identity is that the losers of a political contest believe that they will not be permanent losers; that they will be on the winning side in the not too distant future. In domestic politics in Europe, for example, people who vote for a party that does not become part of the government accept the outcome of an election because they hope that their party will be on the winning side next time. If a section of society feels that it will be permanently on the losing side, the members of this group will not only oppose the government of the day but will also start to oppose the political system as a whole and so will campaign for political reform, as has been the case with regionally concentrated political support, for example in Scotland, Catalonia or Northern Italy.

A similar relationship operates in the EU. The current political majority in the Commission, the Council and the European Parliament is on the centre-right, which means that the current policies of the EU are in a more free market direction. Without open democratic politics, this particular 'governing coalition' is not recognised by most citizens. So, rather than recognising that the current right-wing policies are the product of this particular governing coalition and would change if a different coalition emerged as the governing majority, those parties and citizens on the losing side in the current policy battles (on the left) believe that free market policies will be a permanent feature of the EU.

This explains why many citizens on the left, particularly in Western Europe, increasingly oppose the whole EU project rather than oppose the current policies of the EU. If these citizens expected that the political majority at the European-level could change in the not too distant future, and that the political leaders that they support would be part of a new governing coalition which could move EU policy outcomes in a slightly more social democratic direction, these citizens would be much more willing to accept the EU system as legitimate. Then, over time, as the European-level majorities shift from the moderate right to the moderate left and back again, a European-wide democratic identity would begin to emerge, as it did at the national level in Europe as well as at the federal level in the United States.

Conclusion: gradually politicise Brussels

There is likely to be greater political conflict in the EU in the coming years. Partly this will be because the indirect redistributional consequences of the internal market, EU social and economic regulations and economic and monetary union will become increasingly apparent. Political conflict will also surface as the EU moves beyond creating an internal market to more explicitly political issues, such as how liberal or regulated the internal market should be, how far the EU should foster labour market and service sector reform, or what should be the economic and social rights of EU migrants and third-country nationals.

Rather than fear this development, if managed properly, more EU politics would enable the EU to tackle the three main problems I have identified. More politics would encourage policy innovation, joined-up policy thinking and the formation of interinstitutional coalitions, which would make it easier for the EU to overcome policy gridlock. More open political arguments would also increase the popular legitimacy of the EU. A more vigorous EU political 'soap opera' would create incentives for the media to cultivate the key personalities in Brussels and to cover European-level policy debates instead of portraying EU politics as battles of 'us versus them'. It would also enable citizens to understand European policy issues, to form opinions about the options available, and in time accept why certain reforms are necessary rather than rejecting any policy change directed from Brussels as illegitimate. And, more EU politics would gradually reduce the democratic deficit. People would begin to recognise the coalition that 'governs' in a particular period. Some people would be excluded from this coalition at any one time, but as the coalition gradually shifts from one side of the political divide to the other and back again, citizens would begin to see the EU as a democratic system similar to their systems 'at home'.

Put together, more politics in the EU is inevitable as the redistributional outcomes of EU policies become more apparent. These outcomes will only be legitimate if there is a competitive political process which creates a mandate for these redistributional consequences.

There are potential dangers of more open EU politics, as the losers may challenge the legitimacy of the winners. However, any emerging EU politics will not be like politics in Westminster, where a party representing a minority of voters can win elections and then impose its policies on the losing majority. Instead, the new EU politics would be severely limited. A governing coalition will have to command broad support across the Commission, the Council and the European Parliament. This coalition would also probably shift issue-by-issue, as different majorities form to enable different pieces of legislation to be passed. Politics in Brussels would also be heavily constrained by the fact that it would be elite-level politics, at least initially. In time, citizens may demand more direct involvement in the pseudo-democratic politics in Brussels. At the moment, though, the EU is probably not ready for mass electoral politics, such as a direct election of the Commission President, as the failure of European Parliament elections to generate a European-wide contest have shown.

So, there is a powerful case for 'limited democratic politics' in the EU; limited by the checks-and-balances of the EU system as well as by the fact that it would not be direct democratic politics. Having made the case for a gradual politicisation of the EU, I will now show that the EU institutions and the politicians in these institutions are ready for this change.

CHAPTER SEVEN

How the EU is ready for limited democratic politics

There are two main prerequisites for limited democratic politics in any polity: (1) an *institutional design* that allows for a publicly identifiable coalition to govern for a limited period; and (2) a pattern of *elite behaviour* where competition over policy and the formation of majorities is commonplace.

On the institutional side, the treaty reforms over the last twenty years have changed the EU from an overwhelmingly consensual system to a slightly more majoritarian one. These reforms were discussed at length in chapter 3, but it is worth summarising the three key changes here. First, QMV in the Council now covers all the main areas of social and economic policy, from creation and regulation of the internal market to common environmental and social standards to issues of immigration and the free movement of persons. Second, the European Parliament now has co-equal power with the Council under the co-decision procedure in almost all areas of social and economic legislation. Third, the introduction of QMV in the European Council for electing the Commission President and the Commission, who then have to pass a majority vote in the European Parliament, means that the Commission is now chosen by a coalition of governments and MEPs.

As a result of these reforms an EU version of 'government-opposition' politics is now possible. A particular coalition of governments in the Council and political parties in the European Parliament have the power to appoint 'their' Commission President, who can then allocate the key Commission portfolios to the allies of his or her supporting coalition. This governing team can then put together a multi-annual programme of legislative activity, where the key pieces of legislation have a good chance of being adopted because the same majorities in the Council and Parliament that appointed the Commission are required to pass legislation under the co-decision procedure. Invariably, the coalition of governments and parties will shift issue-by-issue as the subject of the legislation changes. Nevertheless, the institutions are already in place for a particular majority coalition to govern at the European level, at least during the early period of a Commission's term in office.

One interesting aspect of the new EU politics is that the political make-up of the Council changes as national governments are replaced in national elections. Far from seeing this as a negative aspect, this gradual change in the make-up of the Council is a positive limitation on the power of the initial governing coalition. As the Council changes, the Commission will have to broaden its supporting coalition to include key new governments to be able to pass its key legislative initiatives. This would be similar to how bi-partisan deals have to be put together in the US after mid-term congressional elections have produced a Congress controlled by the opposite party to the president.

In other words, politics at the European level would not be like the vicious politics of the Westminster system, where the government and the opposition glare at each other 'two swords' lengths apart' across the floor of the House of Commons. It would be more like the consensual models of coalition government in the Benelux, Scandinavia and Germany or the bi-partisan alliances that emerge in the US when there is divided government between the congress and the president. In either case, the institutions of government (proportional representation in the European systems and separated powers in the US system) ensure that the governing coalition commands broad political support and that any coalition involves the party closest to the average voter.[1] This would be exactly the situation in the EU, where the need to build majorities across three institutions (the Council, the European Parliament and the Commission), would require the governing coalition to be extremely broad, even when similar coalitions dominate all three institutions.

Hence, the institutional prerequisites for limited democratic politics in the EU already exist. However, this sort of politics will not emerge unless the elites inside the institutions – the governments in the Council, the MEPs and parties in the European Parliament, and the commissioners – allow the institutions to work as I have described here. This may seem a fantasy given the highly consensual nature of EU politics and the risk aversion of most politicians! However, the elites have already begun to behave in precisely this way. A genuine party system has emerged in the European Parliament based around left–right coalitions, political contestation is increasingly common in the Council and structured along ideological lines, and relations between the Commission and the other two institutions have become increasingly political.

A genuine party system in the European Parliament

A popular image of the European Parliament is of a chamber divided between groups of national politicians, and where the two largest groups in the Parliament – the European People's Party on the centre-right and the Party of European Socialists on the centre-left – are forced to collude to overcome the national divisions. For example, the Takeover Directive was defeated in 2001 because German MEPs from both left and right voted together against their European parties, and the Services Directive only passed in 2006 because there was a deal brokered between the leaders of the EPP and PES.

Similarly, the spoils inside the Parliament are usually carved up between the EPP and PES, as they were to secure the election of Josep Borrell (a Spanish PES member) as the European Parliament's president from 2004 until 2006 and then Hans-Gert Poettering (a German EPP member) as the president from 2007 until 2009.

However, research on the voting behaviour of the MEPs has revealed a starkly different picture about how politics works inside Europe's only directly elected chamber. In a major piece of collaborate research, Abdul Noury, Gérard Roland and I studied all the recorded ('roll-call') votes in the European Parliament between 1979 and 2006.[2] What we found is that politics in the European Parliament is surprisingly 'normal'. As in all other democratic parliaments, the European Parliament is dominated by ideological conflicts rather than national conflicts, the transnational parties compete with each other to control and shape the policy agenda, and in so doing have become highly internally cohesive.

Voting in the European Parliament is increasingly along party lines and decreasingly along national lines. Figure 7.1 shows the level of voting cohesion of two types of the European parties (such as the EPP and the PES) and the national delegations of MEPs (the MEPs from Britain, Germany, France and so on) in each of the six directly elected parliaments. A 'cohesion score' is a simple measure of how often a particular group of MEPs voted together in a given period. If all the MEPs from a particular political party or from a particular member state voted the same way in every vote in a given period, then the party or member state would have a cohesion score of 1 in that period. Conversely, if the MEPs from a given party or member state were split down the middle, with half voting one way and the other half voting the other way in every vote, the party or member state would have a cohesion score of 0. As a comparison, the Democrats and Republicans in the US Congress have cohesion scores of just

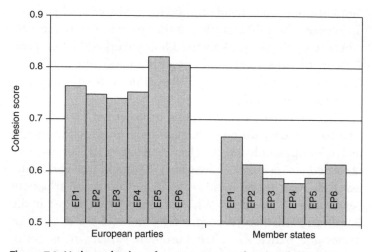

Figure 7.1 Voting cohesion of party groups and national delegations in the European Parliament

Note: These are the 'cohesion scores' of the transnational parties and national groups of MEPs in each European Parliament, where EP1 = 1979–84, EP2 = 1984–9, EP3 = 1989–94, EP4 = 1994–9, EP5 = 1999–2004, EP6 = 2004–6. See the text for the explanation of the meaning of the scores.

Source: Calculated from data used in Hix, Noury and Roland (2005) and Hix and Noury (2006).

over 0.80, while most of the major parties in national parliaments in Europe have cohesion scores close to 0.90.

Voting in the European Parliament is much more along transnational party lines than national lines, and increasingly so. Each MEP is considerably more likely to vote with his or her fellow European party members from other member states than with his or her national colleagues who sit in a different political group. So, a British Labour MEP is more likely to vote with a Spanish Socialist MEP than with a British Conservative MEP. Second, voting along party lines has increased dramatically since 1999. The transnational parties are now as cohesive as the Democrats and Republicans in the US Congress, although they are not quite as cohesive as parties in national parliaments in Europe. Only on extremely rare occasions do MEPs vote along national lines rather than party lines. The reason for the popular conception that the European Parliament is split along national lines is precisely because it tends to be the rare occasions when there is a breakdown in party cohesion that are reported in the press rather than the less exciting day-to-day votes, when MEPs follow the voting instructions of their European party leaderships.

Second, coalitions between the political parties and MEPs in the European Parliament form mainly along left–right rather than pro-/anti-Europe lines. Each political group is more likely to vote with a group that is closer to it on the left–right dimension than a group that is further away. For example, the 'grand coalition' between the PES and the EPP was less common in the 1999–2004 and 2004–9 parliaments than in the 1989–94 and 1994–9 parliaments. This was because these two parties became increasingly divided as the EU agenda shifted to more ideological, left–right, issues, such as reform of working time and services in the internal market or more general economic reform issues. The growing left–right competition between the two biggest groups has meant that the liberal group – known as the Alliance of Liberals and Democrats for Europe in the current parliament – is now in a pivotal position, and can often determine whether a majority coalition forms on the centre-left (for example, on environmental regulation or liberal asylum policies) or on the centre-right (for example, on labour market deregulation or services liberalisation).

The pattern of voting in the fifth directly elected European Parliament, between 1999 and 2004, is captured in Figure 7.2. The figure is produced by 'scaling' the more than 5,000 votes in 1999 to 2004 into a two-dimensional space using an established metric for studying voting in parliaments.[3] Each dot in

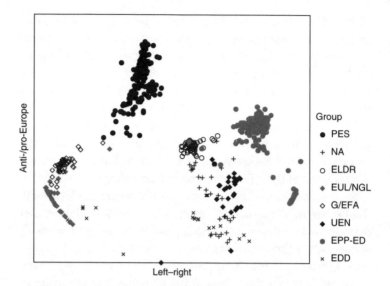

Figure 7.2 Political map of the fifth European Parliament, 1999–2004

Note: This is a NOMINATE plot of the relative locations of the MEPs from their voting records in between 1999 and 2004. Calculated from data used in Hix, Noury and Roland (2007). *Key:*

PES   Party of European Socialists
NA   non-attached MEPs
ELDR   European Liberal, Democratic and Reform Party
EUL/NGL European United Left/Nordic Green Left
G/EFA   Greens/European Free Alliance
UEN   Union for a Europe of Nations
EPP-ED   European People's Party-European Democrats
EDD   Europe of Democracies and Diversities

the figure is an MEP and the distance between any two MEPs indicates how frequently they voted the same way in all the votes. If the two MEPs voted exactly the same way in every vote they are in exactly the same place, whereas if they voted on opposite sides they are on opposite sides somewhere on the edges of the square.

The figure illustrates several aspects of politics inside the European Parliament. First, the main dimension of voting in

the European Parliament is the left–right, where the radical
left, green and socialist MEPs (in the EUL/NGL, G/EFA and
PES groups, respectively) are on the left on this dimension, the
Christian democrat and conservative MEPs (in the EPP-ED and
UEN groups) are on the right, and the liberals (in the ELDR
group) are in the centre. This left–right in the European
Parliament is similar to the left–right in the domestic arena,
where MEPs and parties on the left tend to vote for higher levels
of EU social and environmental regulation, more EU spending,
and more liberal EU migration policies, and MEPs and parties
on the right tend to vote for lower levels of EU social and environmental regulation, less EU spending, and more restrictive
EU migration policies.[4] The left–right dimension explains
about 60 per cent of the voting behaviour of the MEPs. The
second dimension seems to relate to pro-/anti-Europe policy
positions, where the more anti-European parties (the EDD and
EUL/NGL) are at the bottom of the figure and the more
pro-European parties (the PES and EPP-ED) are at the top.
However, the pro-/anti-Europe dimension only explains about
10 per cent of voting behaviour in the European Parliament.

Second, the tightness of the clusters of MEPs shows the high
level of cohesion of the European parties. Interestingly, the main
political groups are more cohesive on the left–right dimension
than on the pro-/anti-Europe dimension (as shown by the
smaller variance in the locations of MEPs on the first dimension
in the figure than on the second dimension). This consequently
gives the party leaders in the European Parliament a strong
incentive to compete on left–right issues rather than pro-/anti-
Europe issues, by couching issues before the parliament in
terms of how far and fast the European economy should be
reformed rather than in terms of the speed of European integration or the powers of the EU relative to national governments.

Third, the relative positions of the party clusters reveal the
types of coalitions that form in the European Parliament. The

distance between the PES and EPP MEPs shows that these two groups do not vote together all the time. In fact, these two groups voted against each other in 31 per cent of the votes in the 1999–2004 period (bear in mind that many votes in the European Parliament, as in all parliaments, are on procedural issues, where there is usually a large coalition in support of an issue).[5] The location of the liberal (ELDR) group between these two groups shows that this group voted in approximately equal proportions with the two largest groups: 74 per cent of the time with the PES and 71 per cent of the time with the EPP. This meant that the liberals were often pivotal in determining whether a centre-left majority emerged (between the PES, EUL/NGL, G/EFA and the ELDR) or a centre-right majority emerged (between the EPP-ED, UEN and the ELDR).

So, politics inside the European Parliament is essentially 'democratic' in that it is highly competitive and the coalitions between the MEPs and European parties are based on the left–right dimension of politics, which is the dominant dimension of politics throughout the democratic world. This democratic politics in the European Parliament has developed as a result of the increased powers of the European Parliament. As the power of the European Parliament has increased, there has been an increased incentive for MEPs with similar policy preferences to organise together to try to shape EU policy outcomes via the European Parliament. There are still significant ideological divisions inside the main political groups, for example between the French Socialists and British Labour MEPs in the PES or between the German Christian Democrats and British Conservatives in the EPP-ED. However, on issues relating to the regulation of the internal market and the reform of the European economy, these MEPs often find that they have more in common with their ideological brethren from other member states than with their political opponents from their own member states. This has enabled the party leaders in the European Parliament to become powerful figures, leading their troops into battle each week in Brussels or Strasbourg.

What is missing, however, is a clear connection between this emerging democratic politics inside the European Parliament and how citizens behave in European Parliament elections. As we saw in chapter 5, citizens do not vote in European Parliament elections to influence which parties form the majority in the European Parliament, and there are few incentives for national parties to treat European Parliament elections as anything more than part of national electoral politics. This might change if there were more at stake in European Parliament elections, as I shall discuss in the next chapter. In the meantime, what is striking is how politics inside the Council is beginning to evolve in a similar direction to politics inside the European Parliament.

Growing ideological battles in the Council

Studying voting in the Council is more difficult than studying voting in the European Parliament as decision-making in the Council is less transparent than decision-making in the European Parliament. Also, most decisions in the Council are made by a consensus rather than by a formal vote, even when a decision could be adopted by a qualified-majority vote. This does not mean necessarily that most issues in the Council command unanimous support amongst the governments. What often happens is that the governments that expect to be on the losing side agree to support the position of the likely majority rather than allow a vote to be taken. This is known as a consensus 'in the shadow of a vote'.[6] Governments have a strong incentive to behave in this consensual way. This is because they are responsible for implementing most EU legislation and it will be difficult for a government to persuade its

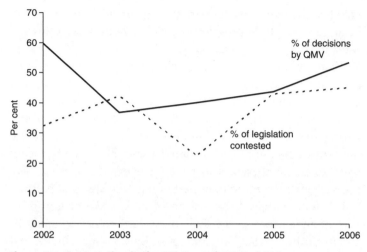

Figure 7.3   Contestation in the EU Council, 2001–2006

Note: The graph shows the percentage of Council legislative decisions in a year that were taken by qualified-majority vote (QMV) rather than unanimity, and the percentage of legislative acts that were adopted with at least one member state either voting against the legislation or registering their opposition to the legislation in a formal statement recorded in the Council minutes. Calculated from data in Hagemann and De Clerck-Sachsse (2007).

domestic interest groups and citizens of the value of a bill if the government voted against it when it was passed.

Nevertheless, since the mid 1990s votes in the Council have been recorded, and research has discovered that most governments are increasingly willing to register the opposition to legislation when it is being adopted in the Council. Also, when there are divisions, these tend to be based on ideological differences between the governments rather than on pro-/anti-Europe differences.

Figure 7.3 shows two measures of the level of conflict in the Council: (1) the percentage of legislative decisions between 2002 and 2006 that were adopted by QMV rather than by unanimity; and (2) the proportion of pieces of legislation that were 'contested', where at least one member state either formally voted against the legislation or registered their opposition in a statement in the Council minutes. There was a dip in the volume of legislation adopted by QMV between 2002 and 2003, but then a rise to about 53 per cent of acts adopted in 2006. On average, just under 50 per cent of legislation that passed through the Council was adopted by QMV in this period. Put another way, whether or not divisions are open or hidden in the shadow of a qualified-majority vote, differences between the governments are likely on about half of the business of the Council.

Figure 7.3 also shows that recorded contestation has increased in recent years. In 2002 one or more governments voted against a piece of legislation on just over 30 per cent of occasions. This rose to just over 40 per cent in 2003. There was then a dip in the level of open contestation in 2004. This was because of the enlargement in May 2004 from fifteen to twenty-seven member states, which slowed down EU business dramatically. It did not take long, however, for business as usual to return, as conflict occurred on 43 per cent of bills in 2005 and just over 45 per cent of bills in 2006.

This may seem a relatively low level of conflict compared to the levels observed in the European Parliament or in national parliaments. Also, it is rare for more than two or three governments to register their opposition to the passage of a piece of legislation. However, it should be remembered that there are strong incentives for governments not to reveal that they lost on a particular bill, which means that most Council decisions are taken without a record of which governments were on what side of the vote. From this perspective, it is rather surprising that almost 50 per cent of EU legislation now passes in the Council with at least one government, and occasionally as many as four governments, being in the losing minority in the adoption of the legislation.

For example, in 1995 to 2000 the German government was on the losing side most often, closely followed by Sweden and the United Kingdom.[7] Germany voted against the majority 5 per cent of the time in that period, while Sweden voted against the majority just over 4 per cent of the time and the United Kingdom voted against the majority just under 4 per cent of the time. However, these three member states were rarely on the losing side at the same time. In fact, Germany and the United Kingdom voted on opposite sides more often than any other pair of member states in that period. This is not surprising if one considers that the main issue in the Council in the late 1990s and early 2000s, as a result of the legislative initiatives of the Santer and Prodi Commissions, was how far the internal market should be further regulated, particularly in the area of social policy. The British government was opposed to new EU social regulations while the German government was opposed to watering down existing regulations or opt-outs for the UK. This meant that while the UK was in the losing minority on issues like the rights of part-time and temporary workers, Germany was in the losing minority on issues like allowing the UK an opt-out on working time rules.

This suggests that what determined the voting behaviour of a government in the Council in the late 1990s was its basic left–right policy position, in terms of how far it supported a liberal internal market or a more social market model.[8] In contrast, whether a government was more supportive or more opposed to further European integration, or whether a government was a net recipient or a net contributor to the EU budget, seemed to be less decisive factors. Put simply, left-wing governments tended to vote together, right-wing governments tended to vote together, and the governments that voted against the winning majority in the Council tended to be either on the furthest left (as the Swedish and German governments were in the late 1990s) or on the furthest right (as the British

Conservative government was until 1997). This meant that in the late 1990s, when thirteen of the fifteen governments were on the centre-left, left-wing governments tended to be on the winning side in the Council while right-wing governments tended to be on the losing side.

By mid 2004, however, the balance of power in the Council had shifted to the right, with the left now in a minority. Consistent with the earlier findings about the role of left–right policy positions in voting in the Council, research on voting in the Council after 1999 has shown that as the governments switched from left to right their voting behaviour changed.[9] This is illustrated in figure 7.4. This figure is similar to the plot of voting in the European Parliament, in figure 7.2 above. Here, the distance between any two governments reveals how often they voted the same way or differently. When there was a change of government the first government is indicated with a 1 and the second government is indicated with a 2; for example, the centre-left government in Austria (Aus1) was replaced in 2000 by a right-wing coalition (Aus2), the left-wing government in France (Fra1) was replaced in 2002 by a right-wing government (Fra2), and so on.

Figure 7.4 reveals several things about politics in the Council in this period. The scaling method does not tell us the substantive meaning of the two revealed dimensions. However, the locations of the governments suggests that the main dimension of voting was still the left–right, since most left-wing governments (underlined in the figure) are on the left of the figure while most right-wing governments are on the right of the figure. Also, when a government switched from left to right it generally moved rightwards along the first dimension, as can be seen in the relative positions of the two Belgian governments, the two French governments, the two Portuguese governments, the two Austrian governments, or the two Danish governments. Furthermore, this left–right

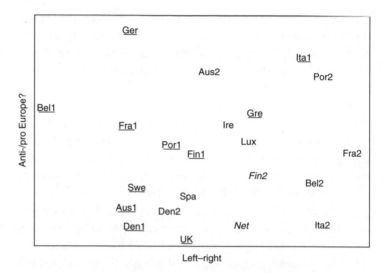

Figure 7.4 Political map of the EU Council, 1999–2004

Note: This is a NOMINATE plot of the relative locations of the governments from their voting records in the Council between 1999 and 2004. The distance between any two governments reveals how often they voted together or against each other in this period. Left-wing or left-led governments are underlined, grand coalitions or governments dominated by centrist parties are in italics, and the others are right-wing or right-led governments.

Source: Calculated from data used in Hagemann (2006).

dimension explains over 50 per cent of vote decisions of governments in this period. In contrast, the second dimension explains less than 10 per cent of vote decisions of the governments. The substantive meaning of this second dimension is not clear, but it looks like it might be related to the speed and extent of European integration as the more pro-European governments are at the top of the figure (such as Germany and Belgium) while the more anti-European governments are at the bottom of the figure (such as the United Kingdom, Denmark and the Spanish Aznar government).

Although it is early days, evidence suggests that open conflicts in the Council have become more frequent since the EU
has enlarged to twenty-five and now twenty-seven states.[10]
With more states, building a consensus is more difficult, and
so more issues are likely to be pushed to a vote. Also, if a government is to avoid being on the losing side in the enlarged EU
it will have to build alliances with like-minded governments
from other member states, and the main basis for any such
alliance is the left–right policy position of each government. In
other words, just as the European Parliament has developed a
genuine party system similar to other democratic parliaments,
the Council has begun to evolve into a more normal legislature, where there is more open conflict and coalitions are
based on underlying ideological preferences.

A political coalition in the Commission

Article 213 of the treaty states that commissioners should 'be
completely independent in the performance of their duties'.
The reality is more complex. Almost all commissioners are
career politicians, with links to national parties, and have
strong views about what types of legislation they would like the
Commission to propose. Also, recent treaty changes have
meant that the Commission is a more political body than it
used to be.

The Maastricht Treaty introduced a right of the European
Parliament to hold a vote on the candidate for Commission
President and to exercise a veto on the proposed Commission
as a whole. Following the treaty, the European Parliament
introduced hearings of each nominated commissioner before
the relevant parliamentary committee, modelled on the US
Senate hearings of nominees to the US president's cabinet.
These changes do not mean that the Commission is beholden
to a particular political majority in the European Parliament,

as governments are in relation to national parliaments. Nevertheless, since the Santer Commission, which was the first Commission to be chosen after the Maastricht Treaty, the Commission, both collectively and individually, has been much more connected and sensitive to the will of the main political parties in the European Parliament.

The Nice Treaty then introduced QMV in the European Council for nominating the Commission President. When the Commission President was chosen by unanimous agreement he (or she!) was inevitably a political moderate, as he (or she) had to be a compromise candidate to satisfy all governments.[11] However, now that the Commission President can be chosen by QMV he (or she) is likely to be more clearly to the left or to the right, as a smaller coalition needs to be put together to support a particular candidate.

The Nice Treaty also introduced one commissioner per member state. When the larger member states had two Commissioners each they usually chose one from the centre-left and one from the centre-right. With one commissioner per member state, almost all governments choose a commissioner from the main party in government. This means that the make-up of the Commission now mirrors the make-up of the Council at the time of the Commission's appointment. As a result, if the Council is dominated by governments on the right (left), the Commission will also be dominated by politicians on the right (left).

These institutional reforms changed the political make-up of the Commission quite dramatically, as Table 7.1 illustrates. In the table, each commissioner is assumed to have the same left–right position as his or her national party. The position of each national party is taken from a survey of experts, where political scientists in each member state were asked to locate each party in their country on the left–right scale.[12] This is not a perfect way of locating the views of each commissioner. For example, on economic issues Michel Barnier was probably not to the right of Fritz Bolkestein. But, these measures do capture how parties have changed their positions over time. For example, Neil Kinnock is measured as slightly to the left of Peter Mandelson, which results from the judgement that the British Labour Party has moved from 0.38 to 0.52 on the left–right scale. As a result, these scores are reasonable approximations of the economic and social policies each commissioner is likely to favour.

The Santer Commission was evenly balanced, with nine conservatives and Christian democrats, two liberals, and nine social democrats. The Prodi Commission had a slight centre-left majority, with ten social democrats, one green and one left-wing Christian democrat (Prodi himself), but was nonetheless a rather broad coalition. Also, Jacques Santer and Romano Prodi were both rather centrist politicians, which resulted from the fact that they were both elected unanimously in the European Council.

In contrast, the first Commission appointed following the introduction of the Nice Treaty was far less balanced. The average member of the Barroso Commission was considerably to the right of the average member of the previous two Commissions. Also, José Manuel Barroso, having been elected by QMV in the European Council, is further from the centre than Santer or Prodi. The political coalition in the Prodi Commission meant that the Commission pursued a moderately centre-left legislative agenda at that time, for example by proposing a series of measures in the social policy field (such as equal treatment on the grounds of race, ethnicity, religion, disability, age and sexual orientation). In contrast, because there is a centre-right majority in the Barroso Commission, the current Commission has proposed more economically liberal legislation.

Furthermore, ever since the Maastricht Treaty, relations between the Commission and the European Parliament have

Table 7.1 Political make-up of the European Commission, 1999–2009					
Santer Commission (1994-9)		**Prodi Commission (1999-2004)**		**Barroso Commission (2004-9)**	
commissioner (member state, party)	LR position	commissioner (member state, party)	LR position	commissioner (member state, party)	LR position
Monika Wulf-Mathies (Ger, SPD)	0.31	Michaele Schreyer (Ger, G)	0.30	László Kovács (Hun, MSZP)	0.32
Manuel Marín (Spa, PSOE)	0.33	Philippe Busquin (Bel, PS)	0.31	Vladimír Špidla (Cze, CSSD)	0.34
Edith Cresson (Fra, PS)	0.34	Pascal Lamy (Fra, PS)	0.34	Joaquín Almunia (Spa, PSOE)	0.38
Anita Gradin (Swe, SAP)	0.34	Erkki Liikanen (Fin, SDP)	0.34	Margot Wallström (Swe, SAP)	0.38
Karel Van Miert (Bel, SP)	0.36	Margot Wallström (Swe, SAP)	0.34	Günter Verheugen (Ger, SPD)	0.39
Ritt Bjerregaard (Den, SD)	0.36	Antonio Vitorino (Por, PS)	0.36	Danuta Hübner (Pol, ind/Left)	0.40
Erkki Liikanen (Fin, SDP)	0.38	Poul Nielson (Den, SD)	0.37		
Neil Kinnock (UK, Lab)	0.38	Günter Verheugen (Ger, SPD)	0.40		
Christos Papoutsis (Gre, PASOK)	0.40	Pedro Solbes Mira (Spa, PSOE)	0.41		
Emma Bonino (Ita, Rad)	0.46	**Romano Prodi (Ita, Dem)**	**0.43**		
		Neil Kinnock (UK, Lab)	0.47		
		Anna Diamantopoulou (Gre, PASOK)	0.50		
Martin Bangemann (Ger, FDP)	0.51	Viviane Reding (Lux, PCS)	0.61	Markos Kyprianou (Cyp, DIKO)	0.51
Pádraig Flynn (Ire, FF)	0.53	Franz Fischler (Aus, ÖVP)	0.62	Peter Mandelson (UK, Lab)	0.52
		David Byrne (Ire, FF)	0.65		
Jacques Santer (Lux, PCS)	**0.56**	Loyola de Palacio (Spa, PP)	0.66	Joe Borg (Mal, PN)	0.57
		Mario Monti (Ita, FI)	0.68	Dalia Grybauskaite (Lit,	0.57

Commissioner	LR position
Hans van den Broek (Net, CDA)	0.59
João de Deus Pinhiero (Por, PSD)	0.60
Franz Fischler (Aus, ÖVP)	0.61
Mario Monti (Ita, FI)	0.68
Frits Bolkestein (Net, VVD)	0.69
Chris Patten (UK, Con)	0.69
ind/centre	0.69
Marcelino Oreja (Spa, PP)	0.72
Michel Barnier (Fra, RPR)	0.72
Leon Brittan (UK, Con)	0.74
Yves-Thibault de Silguy (Fra, RPR)	0.77
Olli Rehn (Fin, KESK)	0.58
Louis Michel (Bel, MR)	0.62
Viviane Reding (Lux, PCS)	0.64
Charlie McCreevy (Ire, FF)	0.65
Janez Potočnik (Slv, ind/centre)	0.65
Andris Piebalgs (Lat, LC)	0.67
José Manuel Barroso (Por, PSD)	**0.68**
Benita Ferrero, Waldner (Aus, ÖVP)	0.70
Jacques Barrot (Fra, UMP)	0.70
Mariann Fischer Boel (Den, V)	0.74
Stavros Dimas (Gre, ND)	0.77
Franco Frattini (Ita, FI)	0.77
Neelie Kroes (Net, VVD)	0.81
Ján Figel' (Slk, KDH)	0.85
Siim Kallas (Est, Ref)	0.96

LR position = left–right position of each commissioner's national party in the relevant period. These positions are based on judgements by political scientists about the location of parties on a scale from 0 (most left) to 1 (most right), see Benoit and Laver (2006) and Marks (2007).

been highly politicised. The Santer Commission was the first Commission to be formally invested by the European Parliament and was also the first Commission to be effectively removed by the European Parliament, in May 2009. There were four key votes in the European Parliament on the Santer Commission: the two investiture votes (on Santer and the Commission as a whole) and two censure votes, as table 7.2 shows.[13] A third censure vote would have been held in May 1999, but the Commission resigned before this vote could take place.

The first vote took place in the first plenary session of the newly elected parliament in July 1994. Many socialist MEPs were furious about the secret horse-trading that had secured Santer's nomination, after John Major (the British Conservative prime minister) had threatened to veto Jean-Luc Dehaene or Ruud Lubbers because they were too Euro-federalist. The socialists also argued that a centre-left politician should be appointed because the Commission President now required the approval of the European Parliament and the socialists were the largest group in the chamber following the June 1999 elections. Despite the opposition of the socialists, Santer narrowly passed the investiture vote, by 260 votes to 238. The vote was broadly along party lines rather than national lines, with right-wing MEPs supporting Santer and left-wing MEPs voting against him – although several socialist MEPs from parties in government voted in favour of Santer, on the instructions of their party leaders, who had supported Santer in the European Council.[14]

Once the other members of the Commission had been nominated it became apparent that the Santer Commission would be a broad coalition. So, in the vote on the investiture of the Commission, the three centre-right parties who had backed Santer were joined by the next two groups on the left–right spectrum, the liberals and the socialists. Only the three small groups to the left of the socialists (the regionalists, greens and radical left) and the anti-Europeans remained outside the broad pro-Commission coalition in the European Parliament. But this broad coalition began to crumble in late 1996, following the Commission's mishandling of the crisis surrounding Bovine Spongiform Encephalopathy (BSE) and the resulting ban on the export of British beef. The European Parliament set up a Committee of Inquiry, which issued a report that severely criticised the Commission. Several MEPs tabled a motion of censure, which was defeated by 188 votes in favour to 326 against. The majorities in the initially pro-Commission parties all voted against the censure, but seven EPP and seventeen socialist MEPs voted in favour, against their European parties' positions.

A much deeper crisis then developed in 1998. Following allegations of mismanagement and nepotism, the European Parliament refused to discharge the 1996 budget and established a Committee of Independent Experts to investigate the allegations. Seventy-one MEPs tabled a motion of censure, which was defeated by 232 in favour to 293 against. This was the largest number of MEPs that had ever voted in favour of censuring the Commission. Also, in the vote two of the initially pro-Commission groups (the liberals and the Gaullists) joined the anti-Commission camp and there was a significant split in both the EPP and socialist groups.

The Committee of Independent Experts issued its report on 15 March 1999, concluding that there had been 'instances of fraud, irregularities or mismanagement'.[15] The report was leaked to the Commission the day before its official release, and Santer immediately called a meeting of the full Commission. Shortly before 1 a.m. the next morning the Commission resigned *en masse*. A key factor in the decision to resign was a statement by Pauline Green, the leader of the socialist group, that the socialist group had changed its position and would now

Table 7.2 Four key votes in the European Parliament on the Santer Commission

	Investiture of Santer as president (21 July 1994)			Investiture of the whole Commission (18 January 1995)			Censure vote on the BSE crisis (20 February 1997)			Censure vote on mismanagement (14 January 1999)		
	Yes	No	Abst.	Yes	No	Abst.	Yes	No	Abst.	Yes	No	Abst.
Political group												
Greens	1	17	2	1	21	0	19	0	2	25	0	0
Radical left	0	21	0	0	14	16	25	0	0	18	3	0
Regionalists	0	18	0	0	12	1	12	3	2	4	13	2
Socialists	45	140	5	177	28	9	17	140	5	37	159	2
Liberals	8	24	6	31	4	13	4	26	2	32	6	0
European People's Party	152	0	1	159	9	4	7	138	2	70	91	21
Gaullists	22	0	1	19	0	3	5	15	1	14	11	2
Italian conservatives	26	0	0	22	1	0						
Anti-Europeans	0	7	8	0	0	14	12	3	0	14	0	0
Non attached MEPs	6	11	0	8	14	0	17	1	1	18	10	0
Member state												
Luxembourg	6	0	0	6	0	0	0	6	0	0	6	0
Spain	49	7	2	54	0	9	11	41	1	1	52	0
Greece	19	4	0	19	2	2	2	10	1	6	11	3

Italy	42	23	1	53	6	7	5	17	0	9	58	0
Ireland	12	3	0	11	3	0	2	7	0	3	11	0
Portugal	17	5	3	17	3	5	6	13	3	5	19	0
Finland				10	4	1	3	11	0	3	9	3
Denmark	7	2	5	11	0	5	2	8	0	9	4	0
United Kingdom	19	67	0	70	9	6	0	71	5	20	57	3
Austria	10			17	3	1	5	14	0	11	10	0
Netherlands		19	2	20	3	8	1	26	1	13	8	7
Sweden				20	1	1	7	9	0	13	6	2
Germany	48	44	3	61	34	2	8	71	2	86	6	0
Belgium	7	17	1	17	7	07	9	14	0	14	8	3
France	24	47	6	31	28	13	57	8	2	39	28	6
Total	**260**	**238**	**23**	**417**	**103**	**60**	**118**	**326**	**15**	**232**	**293**	**27**

Cohesion

Political groups		.75			.74			.77			.64	
Member states	.56	.56			.63			.68			.56	

The political groups are sorted from left to right, except for the anti-European group and the non-attached MEPs. The member state delegations are sorted from the most pro-Commission delegation to least pro-Commission delegation, based on their voting behaviour in these four votes. The cohesion scores are the mean scores for the political groups and delegations.

Source: Hix, Noury and Roland (2007).

vote for censure. With the socialist group switching to the anti-Commission coalition, it was clear that a censure motion would pass the required two-thirds majority threshold. Santer consequently persuaded his colleagues to resign rather than be sacked by the European Parliament.

In other words, government-opposition politics between the Commission and the parties in the European Parliament arrived with the Santer Commission. The initially broad left–right coalition that invested the Santer Commission gradually eroded to a rump centre-right minority. The left-wing parties were also aware that the make-up of the Council had shifted, as several right-wing governments had been replaced by left-wing governments. This meant that the next Commission would most likely have a centre-left majority.

However, after the appointment of the Prodi Commission, the centre-right emerged as the majority in the European Parliament after the June 1999 elections, with the EPP as the largest group. Government–opposition politics between the Commission and the Parliament continued, but unlike the Santer Commission, which started off with an oversized supporting coalition in the European Parliament, the period of the Prodi Commission was one of 'divided government': with a centre-left majority in the Commission facing a centre-right majority in the European Parliament. The socialists behaved like a minority governing party, supporting virtually all the Commission's initiatives, while the EPP, which was dominated by the German CDU (which did not have a commissioner), behaved like the main opposition party.

The political dynamic switched again with the Barroso Commission, to a system of more clearly 'unified government'. This time, a centre-right majority existed in both the Commission and the European Parliament. The majority in the socialist group opposed the Barroso Commission and its policy initiatives right from the start. The socialist group was instrumental in forcing Barroso to withdraw his initial team of commissioners in October 2004, as described in chapter 3. Then, in January 2005 the socialist group also tried to stop the European Parliament approving the Commission's first work programme.

Overall, since the Santer Commission, relations between the Commission, on one side, and the Council and the European Parliament, on the other side, have become increasingly political. Then, as a result of the Nice Treaty, which introduced one commissioner per member state and QMV in the European Council for electing the Commission, the Commission is likely to be a less broadly based coalition. If battles between the Commission and the European Parliament were fierce under the Santer Commission, which was a politically moderate executive, they are likely to become more ferocious in the future, as the Commission will inevitably be the product of a smaller coalition of governments and MEPs.

Conclusion: the EU is ready for more open democratic politics

So, the institutional and behavioural prerequisites for limited democratic politics in the EU already exist. On the institutional side, as a result of the treaty reforms since the 1980s, a broad majority coalition can dominate EU policy-making. A coalition of governments in the Council and political parties in the European Parliament has the potential to appoint a clearly left-wing or right-wing Commission President and then pass the legislative proposals of the Commission. This is how politics works in all democratic systems and is how politics could work at the European level.

On the behaviour side, exactly this sort of politics is beginning to emerge within and between the EU institutions. This is most clear in the European Parliament, where a genuine party system has evolved since the first direct elections in 1979, politics in the chamber is dominated by left–right splits, and political parties act cohesively to influence policy outcomes. Political competition is also developing in the Council, where governments are increasingly willing to vote against the majority, and splits are based on ideological rather than national divisions. And, relations between the Commission and the other two institutions began to be politicised in the mid 1990s with the Santer Commission and continued to be highly political during the Prodi and Barroso Commissions, as divided majorities gave way to a unified centre-right majority across all three institutions.

Despite this emerging politics in Brussels, two elements are missing. First, there is very little coordination of positions and alliances across the three EU institutions. Informal coalitions emerge issue-by-issue, but there are few incentives for politicians to be bound by these coalitions. Second, there is almost no connection between the emerging political structure in the EU institutions and the attitudes of European citizens. Citizens have very little information about politics in Brussels, and so cannot identify the protagonists and the positions they represent. Also, neither national elections nor European Parliament elections provide arenas for parties to compete on the basis of their positions and alliances in the EU.

Thankfully, though, these two issues can be addressed without further reform of the treaties. What is needed is a set of changes that would increase the incentives for EU politicians to coordinate positions and compete more openly, as I shall now explain.

CHAPTER EIGHT

Encouraging democratic politics in the EU

As I have demonstrated, limited democratic politics, in terms of political battles over the direction of the EU policy agenda, has begun to emerge inside the EU institutions. So far, though, the media, the public and even most domestic political elites are unaware of the new politics in Brussels. For example, few TV news editors or national MPs, let alone private citizens, realise that political parties dominate politics in the European Parliament, or know that splits in the Council are often along ideological lines, or recognise that the Commission has become a more political actor. The public, the domestic media and the political elites will not be able to engage with the new democratic politics in Brussels and accept the winners of the political contests as legitimate unless the emerging politics inside the EU institutions is more transparent and clearly understandable.

The connection between the emerging politics within each of the institutions is also weak. For instance, splits in the Council are only coincidently related to splits in the European Parliament. With so many checks-and-balances, cross-institutional coalitions will always have to be constructed on an issue-by-issue basis. Nevertheless, there could be a core alliance across the three institutions which adds partners depending on the issue and the circumstances. This sort of alliance building would enable the EU to overcome policy grid-lock. It would also make the EU more democratically account-able, as it would allow the media, domestic politicians and citizens to identify the members of the core governing alliance and understand what they stand for.

To encourage more transparent and coordinated politics in Brussels there must be greater incentives for elites inside the European Parliament, the Council and the Commission to compete more openly and to link the emerging coalitions across the institutions. This does not require further treaty reforms, and treaty reforms alone would not necessarily change the way political elites behave. What is needed is to change some of the informal practices and formal rules of procedure that govern the way the EU institutions works.

European Parliament: from a fully-proportional to a winner-takes-more model

The key challenge for the European Parliament is how to link the emerging democratic politics inside the institution to citizens' choices in European Parliament elections. As we saw in chapter 5, European Parliament elections are mainly about national issues and not about the EU policy agenda or who should be the largest party in the European Parliament. Communication between the European Parliament and the national media could be improved – for example, through the new European Parliament webTV channel. However, an improved communication strategy alone will not really change the way European Parliament elections work. The problem is that there are very few incentives for national parties and the media to see European Parliament elections as anything other than secondary national contests.

One of the main reasons why European Parliament elections do not work is that policy-making power inside the European Parliament is allocated on a proportional rather than a competitive basis.[1] There is an election amongst the MEPs for the president of the European Parliament. In practice, however, the two largest groups in the Parliament, the EPP and the PES, invariably agree to split the office between them, so that one has the presidency for the first half of the five-year term and the other party has it for the second half. Similarly, there is an informal agreement between all the political groups that committee chairs are assigned in proportion to the size of the political groups.

On the positive side, this proportional way of allocating policy-making power inside the European Parliament means that no one political group dominates the assembly and every political party has some influence over policy outcomes. For example, even the greens and the radical left have committee chairs in the current parliament.

On the negative side, though, the highly proportional method of allocating power means that there is very little at stake in European Parliament elections. European Parliament elections are now held by a system of proportional representation in every member state. This ensures that the average member of the European Parliament is unlikely to change very much from one election to the next and that no political group is likely to capture more than 50 per cent of seats in the Parliament. This is a good thing, as it ensures a fair representation of all the main national political parties. However, when a proportional electoral system is combined with a highly proportional method of allocating powers inside the European Parliament, any change in the make-up of the Parliament that might result from the elections has almost zero impact on policy outcomes at the European level.

For example, in the June 1999 elections the EPP replaced the PES as the largest group in the European Parliament. In electoral terms this was a major change. However, it had very little impact on the policy agenda of the European Parliament because the EPP still had to share the presidency with one of the other political parties in the chamber (with the liberals in

1999–2004 and the socialists in 2004–9) and the system for assigning committee chairs meant that the EPP only gained one more committee chair in the 1999–2004 Parliament than it had in the previous Parliament.

So, despite a dramatic electoral shift, with such a highly proportional system for allocating power inside the European Parliament, the elections had virtually no impact on the direction of the EU policy agenda. As a result, it is probably rational for voters to treat European Parliament elections as national rather than European contests, as these elections are likely to have a bigger impact on national politics (such as the outcome of the next national elections) than on the balance of power at the European level.

Nevertheless, if the key offices inside the European Parliament were allocated on a less proportional basis, the stakes would be considerably higher and there would be a much clearer connection between voters' choices in European Parliament elections and the direction of the EU policy agenda. The European Parliament does not need to be, and should not be, like the US Congress or the British House of Commons, where the winner-takes-all principle produces viciously adversarial politics and means that the party that wins an electoral plurality dominates policy-making. However, the European Parliament could be more like the Scandinavian, Benelux or German parliaments, which have proportional electoral systems but allocate internal offices via what can be described as a winner-takes-more system. Under this system, the largest party has more power inside the parliament than the next largest party, and so on. This provides strong incentives to be the largest party, and so encourages highly competitive elections and also the construction of broad coalitions which have a chance of commanding a majority in the parliament. As a result, the winner-takes-more allocation of legislative power in these systems allows for a clear connection between electoral choices and policy outcomes.

In concrete terms, a winner-takes-more system could be established by two relatively minor changes to the way the European Parliament works. First, *the president of the European Parliament could be elected for a five-year term rather than a two-and-a-half year term.* This would immediately get rid of the 'horse-trading' over this post between the two largest parties. The EPP and the socialists might try to share the president of the European Parliament over consecutive parliamentary terms. However, such an agreement would be difficult to enforce, as the party leaders in the next parliament would be unwilling to be constrained by an agreement between the party leaders in the previous Parliament.

Hence, the most likely outcome of allowing the president of the European Parliament to be elected for the full five-year term would be that the two biggest groups would put up rival candidates for the post and would then try to put together a majority-commanding coalition with the smaller parties in support of their candidate. These alliances would probably involve promising committee chairs or rapporteurships to the smaller groups in return for their MEPs supporting the candidate for the president from one of the bigger groups. The result would be an identifiable majority coalition behind the president of the European Parliament for the full-term of office of the parliament.

Second, *European Parliament committee chairs could be allocated on a winner-takes-more basis rather than on a purely proportional basis.* Chairs of committees are powerful figures in the European Parliament, and can influence EU policy in the area covered by their committee. For example, committee chairs are leading figures in legislative negotiations with the Council under the co-decision procedure. If more committee chairs were allocated to the largest parties, this would give the main parties more power to influence EU policy outcomes. In addition, with extra rewards for being a larger party, there would be stronger incentives for the parties to expand their membership and so build broader majority-winning alliances rather than narrow ideological coalitions.

The current method for allocating committee chairs in the European Parliament, known as d'Hondt, is described in Box 8.1. This method produces a broadly proportional allocation of chairs, with a slight boost for the larger parties. For example, as table 8.1 shows, when the twenty-two committee and sub-committee chairs were reallocated in January 2007 (in the middle of the current parliamentary term), the EPP had 35 per cent of the MEPs and won 41 per cent of the chairs, the socialists had 28 per cent of the seats and won 32 per cent of the chairs, the liberals had 13 per cent of the seats and won 13 per cent of the chairs, and the three parties with just over 5 per cent of the seats won one chair each.

There are at least two ways of allocating committee chairs on a winner-takes-more basis: (1) the 'winners' bonus' method, for example by giving the first five committee chairs to the largest party and then allocating the remaining chairs by the standard d'Hondt method; and (2) the 'modified d'Hondt' method, where the initial points of a party are divided by an additional 0.5 instead of 1 each time a chair is allocated, as box 8.1 explains.

As table 8.1 shows, the 'winners' bonus' method would have increased the number of chairs won by the EPP in January 2007 by three, and reduced the number won by the socialists by two and the liberals by one, while the three smaller parties would each have kept a committee chair. Under the 'modified d'Hondt' method, in contrast, the three smaller parties would have lost their chairs, while the EPP would have won two additional chairs and the socialists would have won one additional chair. Either way, with just over 35 per cent of the MEPs, the EPP would have controlled about 50 per cent of the key policy-making positions in the European Parliament.

Furthermore, either of these two alternative methods would have enabled the largest party to control more of the important committee chairs, as table 8.2 shows. Here, the committees are ranked on the basis of which committees were chosen by each party under the standard d'Hondt method applied in January 2007. Under the 'winners' bonus' method, the EPP would have controlled all of the powerful legislative committees. Under the 'modified d'Hondt' method, these key positions would still have been split between the two biggest parties, but together these two parties would have dominated the main positions, while the third largest party would only have captured the eighth, thirteenth and nineteenth ranked chairs.

In addition to these two main changes, several other things could be changed along the same lines. For example, legislative rapporteurs (the MEPs who draft the amendments to EU bills) could be assigned on a winner-takes-more basis, perhaps following the way committee chairs are assigned. The agenda of the plenary sessions and speaking time in the plenary could be organised differently, to allow the larger parties to have a more dominant control over the proceedings. And, monthly set-piece debates could be organised, where the leaders of the two largest parties 'face-off' against each other and the Commission President in front of the media.

Although these might seem relatively minor changes to the allocation of power inside the European Parliament, their effect on the way European Parliament elections work would almost certainly be quite dramatic. Which European party 'won' the elections would matter for the first time, as being the largest party would enable the members of that party to control the key policy-making positions inside the chamber and so influence the direction of the EU policy agenda and the legislative outputs of the EU. This would have two important effects. First, it would force national parties to change the way

Box 8.1 The d'Hondt method for allocating committee chairs

The d'Hondt method is a divisor method for allocating seats in parliaments/committee chairs in proportion to a party's share of electoral votes/parliamentary seats (the method is named after the Belgian mathematician Victor d'Hondt). The method works as follows. Each party starts with a number of points equivalent to its seats. The party with the largest points is awarded the first chair, and can choose whichever chair it wants, and its points total is then divided by two. The party with the largest remaining points wins the next chair. Each time a party wins a chair, its initial points total is divided by the number of chairs it has plus one. This is illustrated in the example in Table A.

Table A The standard d'Hondt method

No. of Seats	Party A 40	Party B 31	Party C 15	Party D 9	Party E 5
Chair 1	_40_	31	15	9	5
Chair 2	20	_31_	15	9	5
Chair 3	_20_	15.5	15	9	5
Chair 4	13.33	_15.5_	15	9	5
Chair 5	13.33	10.33	_15_	9	5
Chair 6	_13.33_	10.33	7.5	9	5
Chair 7	10	_10.33_	7.5	9	5
Chair 8	_10_	7.75	7.5	9	5
Chair 9	8	7.75	7.5	9	5
Total	4 chairs	3 chairs	1 chair	1 chair	0 chairs
Per cent of chairs	44.4%	33.3%	11.1%	11.1%	0.0%

In the example, each party has the number of seats shown in the second row of the table, with a total of 100 seats. There are nine committees in the parliament. The chair each party wins is indicated in italics and underlined. The first chair is awarded to Party A, as the largest party, and its initial points total of 40 is then divided by 2, to 20. Party B then wins the second chair as it now has the largest remaining total and its starting points total of 31 is then divided by 2, to 15.5. Party A then wins the third chair, as 20 is the largest remaining number, and its points total is now down to 13.33 (the initial 40 divided by 3). And so on. In the end, Party A wins 4 chairs, and gets the first, third, sixth and eighth picks. Party B wins 3 chairs, and gets the second, fourth and seventh picks. Parties C and D each win 1 chair, and get the fifth and ninth picks, respectively. And, Party E wins no chairs. Overall, the number of chairs each party receives is broadly proportional to its seat-share, although there is a slight boost for the largest two parties.

The divisor can be modified to reduce or increase the bias towards the larger parties. For example, if the divisor is increased by 0.5 instead of 1.0 each time a party wins a chair, the largest parties are significantly better off. This is illustrated in Table B. With this modification, Party A wins 5 chairs instead of 4 and although Party C still wins 1 chair, it has the ninth pick instead of the fifth pick.

Table B A modified d'Hondt method

	Party A	Party B	Party C	Party D	Party E
No. of Seats	40	31	15	9	5
Chair 1	_40_	31	15	9	5
Chair 2	26.67	_31_	15	9	5
Chair 3	_26.67_	20.67	15	9	5
Chair 4	20	_20.67_	15	9	5
Chair 5	_20_	15.5	15	9	5
Chair 6	_16_	15.5	15	9	5
Chair 7	13.33	_15.5_	15	9	5
Chair 8	13.33	12.4	_15_	9	5
Chair 9	_13.33_	12.4	10	9	5
Total	5 chairs	3 chairs	1 chair	0 chairs	0 chairs
Per cent of chairs	55.6%	33.3%	11.1%	0.0%	0.0%

they campaign in the elections, explaining to their voters that the election outcome would matter in terms of what policies the EU would enact in the next five years.

Second, it would probably lead to a realignment of the parties in the European Parliament, as there would be strong incentives to build broader coalitions that are more likely to emerge as the largest group. As a result of this alliance-building process, the winning team of parties and MEPs would be much clearer to the public. Also, the performance of the previous winners would be a central issue in the subsequent elections. In

Table 8.1 Alternative methods of assigning Committee chairs in the European Parliament

Political group	Group size		Current model (pure d'Hondt)		Winners' bonus method		Modified d'Hondt method	
	MEPs	%	Chairs	%	Chairs	%	Chairs	%
European People's Party-European Democrats	277	35.3	9	40.9	12	54.5	11	50.0
Party of European Socialists	218	27.8	7	31.8	5	22.7	8	36.4
Alliance of Liberals and Democrats for Europe	105	13.4	3	13.6	2	9.1	3	13.6
Union for Europe of the Nations	44	5.6	1	4.5	1	4.5	0	0.0
Greens/European Free Alliance	42	5.4	1	4.5	1	4.5	0	0.0
European United Left/Nordic Green Left	41	5.2	1	4.5	1	4.5	0	0.0
Independence/Democracy Group	24	3.1	0	0.0	0	0.0	0	0.0
Identity, Tradition and Sovereignty Group	21	2.7	0	0.0	0	0.0	0	0.0
Non-attached members	13	1.7	0	0.0	0	0.0	0	0.0
Total	785	100.0	22	100.0	22	100.0	22	100.0

The size of the political groups is as of 12 April 2007. The table includes the chairs of the twenty standing committees as well as the two sub-committees. The current model allocates these committee chairs to the political groups in proportion to each group's number of MEPs, using the d'Hondt method (see the text for an explanation). The 'winner takes more' method allocates the first five chairs to the largest group and the remainder in proportion to each group's number of MEPs, using the d'Hondt method.

Table 8.2 Actual and hypothetical Committee assignment in the European Parliament

Committee		Hypothetical committee rank	Current chair (pure d'Hondt method)	Chair under winners' bonus model	Chair under modified d'Hondt model
ENVI	Environment	1	EPP-ED	EPP-ED	EPP-ED
ECON	Economic and Monetary Affairs	2	PES	EPP-ED	PES
AFET	Foreign Affairs	3	EPP-ED	EPP-ED	EPP-ED
IMCO	Internal Market and Consumer Protection	4	PES	EPP-ED	PES
LIBE	Civil Liberties	5	ALDE	EPP-ED	EPP-ED
BUDG	Budgets	6	EPP-ED	EPP-ED	EPP-ED
EMPL	Employment and Social Affairs	7	PES	PES	PES
AGRI	Agriculture and Rural Development	8	EPP-ED	EPP-ED	ALDE
ITRE	Industry, Research and Energy	9	EPP-ED	PES	EPP-ED
CONT	Budgetary Cortrol	10	PES	ALDE	PES
TRAN	Transport and Tourism	11	ALDE	EPP-ED	EPP-ED
JURI	Legal Affairs	12	EPP-ED	PES	PES
PETI	Petitions	13	UEN	EPP-ED	ALDE
AFCO	Constitutional Affairs	14	PES	EPP-ED	EPP-ED
DROI	Human Rights	15	G/EFA	PES	PES
INTA	International Trade	16	EUL/NGL	ALDE	EPP-ED

Table 8.2 (cont.)

Committee		Hypothetical committee rank	Current chair (pure d'Hondt method)	Chair under winners' bonus model	Chair under modified d'Hondt model
REGI	Regional Development	17	EPP-ED	EPP-ED	EPP-ED
DEVE	Development	18	PES	UEN	PES
PECH	Fisheries	19	ALDE	PES	ALDE
SEDE	Security and Defence	20	EPP-ED	G/EFA	EPP-ED
CULT	Culture and Education	21	PES	EUL/NGL	PES
FEMM	Women's Rights and Gender Equality	22	EPP-ED	EPP-ED	EPP-ED

The 'rank' of the committees is based on the committees each political group chose in January 2007 on the basis of their allocation using the d'Hondt method. I have assumed the same rank order for the hypothetical allocation of committees using the proposed 'winner takes more' method.

time, raising the power stakes inside the EU's only directly elected institution might enable European Parliament elections to gradually evolve from second-order national contests into genuinely first-order European contests.

EU Council: a proper and transparent legislature

The Council used to be a very secretive institution. No longer. As a result of changes in the Amsterdam and the Nice treaties and the agreement at the Seville European Council in June 2002, the Council operates in a far more transparent way than it used to. There is now public access to some Council documents. Debates in the Council are open to the public at certain stages in the legislative process. And, when votes are taken by qualified majority or unanimity, how each government voted is recorded in the Council minutes, which are available via the PreLex legislative tracking service on the EU's website.[2]

The Council also works far more like a normal legislature and less like an intergovernmental body than it used to. In the past, negotiations in the Council used to start with a *tour de table* (tour of the table), where each government minister spoke in turn, explained his or her government's position on the legislation, and proposed some amendments to the Presidency's text. With enlargement to twenty-five and now twenty-seven member states, the *tour de table* is unfeasible as it would take almost all day for each government to speak, explain its position and present its amendments. At the Seville European Council the governments consequently agreed to streamline how the Council scrutinises and amends legislation. First, the member state holding the Council presidency (which rotates between the governments every six months) has the authority to determine which ministers can speak at the meeting, which order they will speak in, and the amount of time they have to speak. Second, governments are required to propose amendments to legislation in writing before a date specified by the Presidency, together with an explanation of the amendments. Third, and most crucially, governments with identical or similar positions on a particular item are expected to propose joint amendments – often called 'composite amendments' in other legislatures – and to choose only one of the governments to present the amendment and speak on behalf of the other governments at the meeting.

So, when making legislation, some Council debates are held in public, the outcome of votes is recorded, together with an explanation of why each government voted a certain way, and governments are expected to present joint amendments and coordinate their positions before meetings. These provisions have improved deliberations and have begun to make the Council work more like a regular legislative chamber. The Council is now quite different to other intergovernmental ministerial bodies, such as the UN Security Council or NATO Ministerial Meetings, where governments meet behind closed doors, votes are rarely taken, and governments do not speak on each others' behalf. Nevertheless, several things could be changed in the way the Council works to encourage the governments to compete in a more open way and to build alliances across policy issues.

First, *all legislative documents of the Council should be publicly available.* Public access to documents in the Council is better than it used to be. The provisional agendas for meetings are now available as are minutes of meetings. Also, certain legislative documents can be obtained on request and if the member state who authored the document gives its approval. However, this is not the same as full public access to legislative documents, which is standard practice in a truly democratic legislature, as in the European Parliament. European citizens, the media, interest groups and national politicians should have access to all legislative documents in the Council, which would include agendas of all meetings, legislative documents proposed by the Presidency, texts of all legislative amendments proposed by the other governments, verbatim reports of the proceedings of every meeting of the Council, and full and complete minutes of meetings, including texts adopted and records of roll-call votes.

One argument against this is that it would be very expensive and take a long time to translate all legislative documents in the Council into all the EU official languages. This is a poor defence. If the European Parliament can do it, then there is no reason why the Council cannot. Also, it may be reasonable for the governments not to make public documents that are not part of the EU legislative process, such as ministerial documents in the General Affairs and External Relations Council relating to Common Foreign and Security Policy. However, there is no justification for keeping documents out of the public realm when they relate to legislative acts, which are debated by our elected representatives and are binding on us as citizens. Until all legislative documents are easily available at the earliest possible moment, on the website of the Council and on the EU's PreLex legislative tracking service, the Council cannot be considered to be a truly democratic legislative chamber.

Second, and related to this first suggestion, *all legislative deliberation in the Council should be open to the public.* Under the rules agreed at the Seville European Council, debates in the Council are open to the public at two stages of the co-decision procedure: (1) during the initial stage, when the Commission presents its initial proposal and in the ensuing debate between the governments; and (2) during the final stage, when the public can see the final vote in the Council on a bill and hear the explanations of how each government votes. The Council advertises which sessions are open and at what times, on its website.

However, Council debates are not open during the first reading of legislation under the co-decision procedure, after the initial debate on the Commission's proposal, which is when the governments get down to the serious business of agreeing a 'common position' on the legislation. Deliberations are not open during the second reading of legislation, when the Council considers the amendments proposed by the European Parliament, nor at third reading, when the Council discusses whether to accept or reject a 'joint text' they have agreed with the European Parliament in the conciliation committee (which meets if the European Parliament and Council still disagree after two readings in each institution). And, debates are not open at any stage of the consultation procedure, which is still used for almost half of all EU legislation. Hence, despite the recent changes, the Council is still probably the most secretive legislative chamber anywhere in the democratic world. One could even go as far as saying that the legislative process in the Chinese National People's Congress is more transparent than the legislative process in the EU Council!

Third, *amendment rights in the Council should be restricted to coalitions of governments,* who for example command a certain number of votes under QMV and a certain number of member states. In normal democratic legislatures, the allocation of agenda-setting rights – in terms of who has the right to propose amendments and under what conditions – is moderately restricted. This avoids what are called 'spoiling amendments', where an actor can derail proceedings by proposing lots of amendments. Restrictions on agenda-setting also prevent random policy outcomes. Above all, moderate restrictions on amendments facilitate coalition-building and transparent decision-making, as it becomes easier to see who has proposed what.

Currently in the Council, the allocation of amendment rights is relatively *ad hoc.* The Presidency organises the agenda, but there are no restrictions on who can propose amendments and how they are then voted on. This provides no incentive for governments to coordinate their behaviour with other governments or build and maintain alliances prior to legislative deliberations. Contrast this with the European Parliament, where at the committee stage, a *rapporteur* is appointed to prepare a report and the 'shadow *rapporteurs*' from the other party groups in the Parliament coordinate with their party members in the committee and propose amendments on behalf of their party. This way, the amendments are restricted and the coalitions in support of the amendments are clear beforehand.

A similar set of rules could exist in the Council. For example, amendments to proposals by the Presidency could only be made by a group of ministers from at least 14 per cent of member states (so, 4 out of the current 27) who together command at least 14 per cent of the votes under QMV (49 votes out of the current 345). This would make legislative deliberations in the Council far more efficient, as the number of amendments would be limited to a few key issues. It would also enable the public to identify the key amendments and which governments are behind which amendment. It would also encourage governments to build alliances. This would initially be on an issue-by-issue basis. But, in time, *ad hoc* alliances might evolve into more stable coalitions.

As we saw in the previous chapter, vote splits in the Council are increasingly on ideological lines. This suggests that emerging alliances in the Council would most likely be between governments with similar partisan and ideological preferences, such as a group of liberal/free market governments (whether conservatives, liberals or reformist social democrats) against a group of more traditional social-market/socialist governments (whether socialist, Christian democrats or greens). Such alliances would enable politics inside the Council to be linked to the existing structure of political competition in the

European Parliament and to the emerging structure of political competition between the Council and the European Parliament, on one side, and the Commission, on the other.

Fourth, *all legislative decisions in the Council should be put to a vote and the outcomes recorded in the minutes.* Although all votes are currently reported in the minutes, very few votes are actually taken. For example, research on voting in the Council reveals that when qualified-majority voting is used, votes are only held about 30 per cent of the time.[3] The other 70 per cent of the decisions are reached by consensus without a vote taking place. One could argue that if all votes were recorded, the minutes would simply state that a vote was unanimous in these consensual decisions. However, even if there were a unanimous agreement, this is important information, in and of itself. More significantly, if all votes are recorded, as is the case in most democratic legislatures, it is likely that governments will start to behave differently. Recording all votes will allow the public, the media and interest groups to track votes in the Council more closely. If governments know that they are being watched more closely, there will be growing pressure on governments to vote a particular way on a particular issue. This, in turn, will force governments to build alliances for key votes to secure the outcomes they desire.

The beauty of these reforms is that they do not require any changes to the treaty. What is needed is an agreement by the governments to change some of the rules of procedure of the Council and to change the way some of the existing rules are implemented.

Because the Council is composed of ministers and officials from national bureaucracies rather than directly elected politicians, the Council will never be exactly like a normal democratic legislature. However, the Council is the main legislative body in the EU, and when making legislation, there is little justification for the Council to not be more transparent and democratic than

it is now. If all documents were publicly available, if all deliberations were in the open and recorded verbatim, if there were
restrictive amendment rights, and if votes were taken on all
issues, there would be strong incentives for governments to
compete more openly and to build alliances. This would enable
outside actors, in the other EU institutions and in national parliaments, as well as interest groups and the media, to track positions and alignments in the Council more clearly. This, in turn,
would encourage governments in the Council to coordinate
their positions with the parties in the European Parliament and
the political coalition that governs in the Commission, and so
facilitate the creation of cross-institutional alliances.

European Commission: an open contest for the Commission President

The Commission President is the most powerful office in the
EU. The Commission collectively has a monopoly on the initi-
ation of EU legislation, and the Commission President is the
most powerful figure in the team of commissioners. The
Commission President can influence who the governments
nominate as commissioners. He or she allocates portfolios
amongst the commissioners and has the power to reshuffle
the portfolios. The Commission President is responsible for
setting the Commission's policy agenda during its five-year
term and in practice no legislation can be proposed without the
agreement of the Commission President. And, he or she
chairs the weekly meetings of the Commission, and the head
of his or her personal cabinet (group of senior advisors) con-
venes and chairs the weekly meetings of the *chefs de cabinet* of
the commissioners. So, in many respects, the Commission
President is similar to a prime minister in the cabinet government systems at the domestic level: a role Walter Bagehot
famously described as a *primus inter pares* (first among equals).

As discussed in chapter 3, the Commission President used to be chosen by unanimity in the European Council, with no involvement of the European Parliament. Since Maastricht, starting with the appointment of Jacques Santer in 1994, the European Parliament has had a *de facto* right to reject the governments' nominee. And, since the Nice Treaty, starting with the appointment of José Barroso in 2004, the Commission President was nominated in the European Council by QMV before being put to a vote in the European Parliament.

Despite the importance of the post and the changing rules of the investiture procedure, it is often assumed that the Commission President is appointed in a rolling package-deal between the governments. This deal ensures that a president from a big state is followed by one from a small state and a president from the right is followed by one from the left. So, after Roy Jenkins (British, Social Democrat), came Gaston Thorn (Luxembourg, liberal), Jacques Delors (French, social democrat), Jacques Santer (Luxembourg, Christian democrat), Romano Prodi (Italian, left-wing Christian democrat), and José Barroso (Portuguese, conservative).

However, there have always been political battles and coalition-building behind the façade of this rolling package-deal. For example, Delors was only appointed after there had been a bitter battle between Margaret Thatcher and François Mitterrand over the appointment of Claude Cheysson. Santer was the compromise candidate after John Major had threatened to veto Jean-Luc Dehaene. Prodi was appointed after Tony Blair had helped put together a coalition in support of his candidacy amongst the thirteen centre-left governments at that time. And, José Barroso was chosen against Jacques Chirac and Gerhard Schröder, who had openly thrown their weight behind Guy Verhofstadt, the Belgian liberal prime minister.

Also, politics have begun to play a greater role in the appointment of the Commission President for several reasons. First, since the involvement of the European Parliament in the appointment process, the make-up of the European Parliament and the positions of the parties in the European Parliament have started to influence the negotiations between the governments. For example, the leader of the largest group in the European Parliament after the 2004 elections, Hans-Gert Poettering of the European People's Party, made it clear that his group would only support a candidate from the centre-right.

Second, the move to qualified-majority in the European Council for nominating the Commission President has led to more politicians putting their names forward as candidates, as their chances of winning are greater with a lower decision-making threshold. When QMV was first used, in 2004, a large number of politicians came forward. From the right, in addition to Barroso there was Chris Patten, the British conservative commissioner, Wolfgang Schussel, the Austrian chancellor, Jean-Claude Juncker, the Luxembourg prime minister, and Bertie Ahern, the Irish taoiseach. From the centre, in addition to Verhofstadt, there was Pat Cox, the Irish European Parliament president, Anders Fogh Rasmussen, the Danish prime minister, and Peter Sutherland, the Irish chairman of BP and former EU commissioner and WTO secretary-general. And from the left there was Paavo Lipponen, the Finnish prime minister, Antonio Vitorino, the Portuguese commissioner, and Javier Solana, the Spanish high representative for the common foreign and security policy. It was certainly not a foregone conclusion that Prodi's successor would be from the right and a small country, as the rolling package-deal would have suggested.

Furthermore, enlargement from fifteen to twenty-seven member states makes consensus amongst the governments on a single candidate less likely and increases the number of potential candidates. And, as the agenda of the EU has shifted from market-creation to economic reform, who is the Commission president, with the power to propose legislation, has become more politically contentious.

But, despite the growing political battles in the appointment process, the election process has remained behind closed doors rather than out in the open. In the appointment of Santer, John Major's veto of Dehaene and the efforts to find a compromise candidate were conducted in secret conclaves between the governments, which left the media relying on leaks from insiders to follow what was going on. So, when Santer was presented to the European Parliament in July 1994, many MEPs were angry at the way he had been nominated – against the spirit of the new investiture procedure in the Maastricht Treaty, which should have made the appointment process more transparent. Pauline Green, the leader of the socialist group, the largest group at that time, launched the debate on Santer with the following words:

> The European Union is a Union of Member States and people who live in some of the most sophisticated, and most developed countries in the world; countries that pride themselves on their democratic traditions, countries that lecture the world on democratic rights . . . Yet, these same countries are willing to connive at the most squalid, shabby, ill-judged practices to put in place what is essentially the most important position in Europe, the President of the European Commission. The Council makes pious statements about improving openness, democracy, about the need to make Europe more accessible, to bring Europe closer to its people. Then on our television screens it shows us prime ministers and presidents huddled in corners trying to find a candidate acceptable to the majority. In the view of my group this Parliament should refuse to condone a practice which so sullies the democratic process.[4]

In the end, Santer won the vote in the European Parliament by a narrow margin. But, the way he had been nominated, by secretive bargains between the governments, meant that he did not have a strong support base in the European Parliament to protect him when his Commission hit crisis towards the end of its term (as we saw in the previous chapter).

The nominations of Prodi and Barroso were not much better. In a rush to appoint someone after Santer's resignation in May 1999, there was little public discussion about Prodi or other candidates. Then, the appointment of Barroso in 2004 was almost a repeat of the Santer debacle. Tony Blair met privately with Silvio Berlusconi and several prime ministers from the new member states to block Verhofstadt. In return, Chirac and Schröder indicated privately to Bertie Ahern (the chair of the European Council at that time) that they would veto Chris Patten. After failing to agree at the European Council on 17–18 June 2004, despite negotiating late into the night, Ahern held private discussions with all twenty-four other heads of government. After meeting Blair in London, the two premiers faced the press outside No. 10 Downing Street. A correspondent asked who they wanted as the next Commission President, to which they replied: 'No comment'. This was an astonishing statement. Surely we have a right to know who our elected leaders support for the most powerful office in the EU?

The 'election' of the Commission President – and it is an *election*, regardless of the procedure – will not be a democratic process unless it is clear what each of the potential candidates stands for, in terms of what he or she intends to do if elected, and which national government and party leaders back which candidates.

This realisation led several governments, the European Parliament and even the Commission to propose that the current investiture procedure be changed in the proposed EU Constitution: to allow a majority in the European Parliament to nominate, and the European Council to then approve by QMV. Such a reform would immediately make the election more open and political, as each party in the European Parliament would propose a candidate in the European Parliament elections and then try to construct a majority in support of their candidate amongst the newly elected MEPs. But, this proposal did not end up in the failed EU Constitution or in the revised set of reforms agreed in October 2007.

Nevertheless, such a reform may not be necessary to enable a contest to take place, as there is plenty of room to create a contest for the Commission President under the current procedure (where the governments propose by QMV and the MEPs accept or reject by a simple majority). What is needed is for a number of national party leaders, government leaders and party leaders in the European Parliament to take the initiative, to change the way the process works at a political level. This could happen as follows.

First, *groups of national party leaders should declare their support for particular candidates for Commission President before European Parliament elections.* This could be done via the existing transnational party federations, such as the European People's Party, the Party of European Socialists, the European Liberal, Democrat and Reform Party and the European Green Party. These 'Euro-parties' are different from the party groups in the European Parliament: the groups are in effect the 'parliamentary factions' of the Euro-parties. The Euro-parties hold 'leaders' summits' every few months, where the prime ministers and opposition leaders from the national member parties get together, with the leader of their group in the European Parliament and their commissioners, to discuss EU business and common policy concerns. These leaders' summits are perfect vehicles for groups of prime ministers and national parties to propose candidates for the Commission President. As soon as one of the Euro-parties proposes a candidate the others would be under pressure to follow.

Second, once nominated, *the candidates should set out their policy agenda ('manifesto') for their five-year term as Commission*

President. This would allow a debate to take place, as the direction of the EU policy agenda if one or other of the candidates wins would be much clearer. This would also promote joined-up thinking across policy issues, as commitments in one policy area (such as labour market liberalisation) would have to be balanced with commitments in other areas (such as greater investment in research and retraining). And, this would enable the media and the public to hold the Commission and the governments and party leaders who support the winning candidate to account, as it would be clear *a priori* who supported what policy positions when these policies succeed or fail.

Third, *the European Parliament should invite the candidates to hold a live public debate*. A debate would make the candidates more widely recognisable, and enable the media and the public to understand the personal and policy differences between the candidates. The European Parliament is the ideal venue for such a contest. The European Parliament already holds live debates between the candidates for president of the European Parliament. The European Parliament has the media facilities for a debate to be broadcast live on all the main TV channels in Europe and on the internet. And, the European Parliament has the facilities to translate the interventions and questions from an audience simultaneously into all the EU's official languages. More than likely, such a debate and most interventions would be conducted in English with some comments, questions and answers in several other languages, as is the case in the European Parliament president debates.

Finally, once elected, *the manifesto commitments should guide the allocation of Commission portfolios and a multi-annual work programme*. The governments would maintain control over the nomination of the other members of the Commission. But, after a more open contest, the Commission President would have a clearer mandate for the allocation of key portfolios in the Commission to his or her main allies. The Commission President would also have an incentive to set out a multi-annual work programme for his or her term in office, based on the policy commitments in his or her election programme and any compromises that have been made in the election process with other candidates and the governments and party leaders in the European Parliament.

How exactly such a contest for the Commission President might work is elaborated in the scenario in the next chapter. Put simply, even without treaty reforms, if rival candidates were presented before European Parliament elections and then played a role in the election campaigns, the initiative would be taken away from the European Council, as after the elections the heads of government would be under a lot of pressure to formally nominate the candidate of the Euro-party that emerges as the largest group in the newly elected Parliament. In some ways this would be similar to the German system, where federal parties announce candidates for the Federal chancellor before Bundestag elections, and the German president then formally appoints the leader of the largest party in the Bundestag.

The whole process would be more transparent. There would be a clearer connection between citizens, their governments and the Commission. The media would have an incentive to cover the appointment of the most important office in the EU. The public would be able to identify who the Commission President is and what he or she aims to achieve. And, the 'losing side' in a contest for the Commission President would have an incentive to put together an alternative policy package and find a good candidate who could win in the European Council and European Parliament next time round. The result would be a wider public debate about what policies the EU should be adopting and why.

This would change the nature of the Commission, of course, by making it a clearer 'political' body rather than pretending that it is part political executive and part technical bureaucracy. However, the risks of a more open battle for the Commission President would be quite low. The Commission as a whole would still be a broad coalition, as the governments would still control the nomination of the other members of the Commission. The Commission would still be constrained by the checks and balances of the EU system, which mean that any elected Commission President would need a very broad coalition of commissioners, governments and MEPs to be able to pass legislation. And, in many respects, an open contest for the Commission President would simply be a more honest recognition of the reality: that, after the polity-building phase of the EU's development, the Commission is now forced to make explicitly political choices about what social and eco-nomic policies should be pursued in Europe's continental-scale polity.

Having said that, if there is a more open contest for the Commission President there would be a case for removing some of the more technocratic competences from the Commission. Some of the Commission's current compe-tences are meant to produce pareto-efficient rather than redis-tributive outcomes, and so are better made by an independent rather than a political body (as was discussed in chapter 6). For example, if there were a more open contest for the Commission President, the Commission's power to veto cross-border mergers should be delegated to an independent European Cartel Office.

Conclusion: towards identifiable EU politics

A lot can be done to promote limited democratic politics in the EU within the current institutional framework. By allocating agenda-setting powers inside the European Parliament in a less proportional way, the stakes for national and European parties in European Parliament elections would be raised. By fully opening up the legislative process in the Council, interest groups, parties and the media would be able to see what positions are taken by which governments and what coalitions form in the Council. And, by announcing candidates for the Commission President before European Parliament elections, prime ministers and national party leaders would take sides and a more open contest for the most powerful executive office in the EU would result.

These changes would promote more competition between the political elites at the European level, which in turn would have positive benefits for the accountability of the EU and would improve EU policy-making, as was discussed in chapter 6. The political divisions and alliances inside and across the EU institutions would be transparent to national politicians, newspaper and TV editors, interest groups and ordinary citizens for the first time. Coalitions across the EU institutions would start to be linked, as government positions in the European Council, party behaviour in the European Parliament, and who supports which candidate for the Commission President would start to play a role in European Parliament elections and be reported more widely in the media. These developments would strengthen the existing Euro-party organisations, such as the European People's Party and the Party of European socialists, as they would become vehicles for the coordination of alignments within and between the EU institutions. And, as a result, there would start to be public identification of the policy options on the EU table and the winners and losers in the EU political process. In short, there would be democratic politics in the EU for the first time.

It might seem counterintuitive that such developments are possible without new treaty reforms. It is important to bear in mind, however, that how politics works under any constitutional design is determined by the way the formal rules are applied by political actors. For example, in many national constitutions in Europe, the king or queen still formally chooses the prime minister, as they have done for centuries, whereas in practice the prime minister is chosen by the party or coalition of parties that form a parliamentary majority after each election. It is not that constitutions do not matter. Of course they do. But, what is crucial to understand is that all the necessary constitutional provisions for limited democratic politics in the EU are already in place. What is now required is a commitment on the part of the key political actors in the EU – prime ministers, national party leaders and the party leaders in the European Parliament – to fill the existing constitutional shell with some democratic political content.

CHAPTER NINE

A scenario: the 2009 European Commission President contest

To illustrate how a contest for the Commission President would work, imagine the following scenario.

It is 2009, and a new Commission President will be chosen under the procedure set out in the Nice Treaty, which was first used in the appointment of José Barroso in 2004. The European Parliament elections are in June 2009. The heads of government will then meet in the European Council at the end of June to nominate a Commission President, by a qualified-majority vote, if necessary. The governments' nominee will then be put to a vote in the first session of the new European Parliament in July. If the nominee wins a majority in the European Parliament, he or she will take office, along with the other members of the Commission, in November 2009.

In April 2009, the social democrat party leaders meet at the Party of European Socialists (PES) summit and agree that after fifteen years of conservative and liberal Commission Presidents they should do everything they can to ensure that the next Commission President is a social democrat. To maximise their chances they agree to rally behind a single candidate. After intense negotiations they agree to support 'Margot', who is a senior figure in the Swedish social democrats and was the Swedish commissioner in the Prodi and Barroso Commissions.[1] She is well known in the European media and would be the first woman Commission President if appointed. The social democrats agree to organise their European Parliament election campaigns around her candidacy. Even if the social democrat prime ministers do not together command a qualified majority in the European Council in July, if the PES could emerge as the largest party group in the newly elected European Parliament there would be pressure on all the governments to nominate Margot.

With a strong social democrat candidate and a commitment by the social democrat leaders to fight the European Parliament elections around her candidacy, the pressure is on the other European parties to respond. The greens and liberals jump at the chance. The executive committee of the European Green Party, which has thirty national member parties from the EU states, decides to support 'Dany', the leader of the green group in the European Parliament, from the French Green Party. He is a charismatic and popular politician who rose to prominence as the unofficial spokesman of the 'generation of 68'.

The Party of the European Left, which brings together a large number of radical left and ex-communist parties, cannot agree on a common candidate, but urge their member parties to support Dany in the European Parliament elections. The European Free Alliance, of regionalist parties, are split, but their parties who sit with the greens in the European Parliament (such as the Scottish National Party and several Spanish nationalist parties) state that they will also support Dany.

The national party leaders of the European Liberal, Democrat and Reform Party (ELDR) then decide to put forward 'Andrus', the Estonian liberal prime minister, as their candidate. His government has maintained a successful liberal economy, which has been a model for reformist governments in Central and Eastern Europe. His candidacy might also address declining support for the EU in several of the new member states.

The European Democratic Party (EDP), whose MEPs sit with the ELDR MEPs in the Alliance for a Liberal and Democratic

Europe in the European Parliament, discuss whether to support 'Andrus', but cannot agree a united position. The leader of the Italian Partito Democratico, who is the prime minister of a centre-left government, announces that his coalition will support Margot.

At the party leaders' summit of the European People's Party (EPP), the sitting Commission president, 'José', declares that he would like to continue for a second term. The EPP leaders duly endorse his candidacy and commit to campaign in the European Parliament elections to ensure that the EPP group remains the largest group in the European Parliament.

Next, the long-standing Irish taoiseach, 'Bertie', declares his candidacy. The Alliance for a Europe of the Nations (AEN), which brings together several centre-right parties who are more critical of the EU than the EPP (including the Irish, French and Polish conservatives and the Italian national alliance), declare that they will support Bertie. The British and Czech conservative party leaders also lend their support to Bertie. These two parties sit in the European Democrats wing of the EPP-ED group in the European Parliament and prefer Bertie to José, as they are wary of the Euro-federalist tendencies of some of the parties in the EPP.

The leaders of all the major national parties in Europe have now committed themselves to one of these five candidates. The remaining parties, on the extreme right and amongst the various anti-European movements on the right and left, are not prepared to endorse any of these. The UK Independence party urges British citizens to vote for their candidates in the European Parliament elections to declare their opposition to British membership of the EU.

The five main candidates each issue statements of what they would like to do in their five years in office if they become Commission President (see table 9.1). These 'manifestos' cover a wide range of issues on the EU agenda, and each represents a clear and coherent policy package. The candidates then embark on speaking tours throughout Europe, visiting most member states, in an effort to rally support and increase media coverage of their campaigns.

In early June, just over a week before the elections, the European Parliament invites the candidates to participate in a live debate, with short introductory speeches followed by questions from a panel of journalists, academics, interest group representatives and private citizens from each EU member state. The debate is broadcast live by the main TV channels in all the member states and on the internet, on the European Parliament's webTV service. The European Parliament offers its translation services to the national broadcasters, to translate the interventions simultaneously into all the EU official languages. In the end, the candidates make their speeches and most of their interventions in English, although several candidates make an effort to answer some of the questions in French and German.

The European Parliament elections are then held on the second Thursday and the following Sunday in June. Interest in the elections has increased throughout Europe. Some opposition and extremist parties try to use the elections as opinion polls on the performance of the parties in government at the national level, as they have always done. And many citizens respond to these cues, and vote for opposition parties and smaller parties as a protest against their governments or to express their preferences on particular issues, such as environment protection and immigration. However, because of the link between the elections and the contest for the Commission President, a significant proportion of voters recognise the 'European' element of the campaign for the first time. Most of these voters take their cues from the leaders of the parties they usually support in national elections, who have endorsed one or other of the five candidates for Commission President.

Table 9.1 The candidates – from left to right

Name: Member state: Party:	Dany France Green	Margot Sweden Social democrat	Andrus Estonia Liberal	José Portugal Pro-EU conservative	Bertie Ireland EU-critical conservative
Supporters	European Green Party, plus Party of the European Left and left-wing parties in European Free Alliance	Party of European Socialists	European Liberal, Democrat and Reform party, and the European Democratic Party	European People's Party	Alliance for a Europe of the Nations, plus centre-right parties in the UK, Czech Republic, Sweden and Denmark
Policies	• more European-wide social and labour standards	• liberal labour markets for small and medium-sized firms in the service sector	• abolish some EU social regulations, and general derogations for small firms	• derogations for small and medium-sized firms from some EU regulations	• more national derogations from single market rules
	• coordinate national policies to combat unemployment and increase R&D spending	• coordinate national policies to combat unemployment and increase R&D spending	• policies to force member states to deregulate labour markets	• policies to encourage member states to reform labour markets	• no new EU policies, and give some policies back to national governments
	• abolition of the Services Directive	• full implementation of existing Services Directive	• new Services Directive with 'country of origin' principle	• full implementation of existing Services Directive	• abolition of the Services Directive

• no common energy policy	• common energy policy to tackle climate change	• new carbon-trading policy	• common energy policy to tackle climate change	• common energy policy to promote sustainable energy
• open the CAP to the free market, and re-nationalise part of subsidies	• open the CAP to the free market, but keep some subsidies to farmers	• open the CAP to the free market, and re-nationalise part of subsidies	• open the CAP to the free market, but keep welfare support for small farmers	• replace CAP with subsidies for environmental-friendly food production
• abolish EU equal opportunity regulations	• EU policies to promote the family and work-life balance	• non-discrimination on grounds of gender, race and sexual orientation extended	• non-discrimination on grounds of gender, race and sexual orientation extended	• employment quotas for women and ethnic minorities
• suspend Stability and Growth Pact	• maintain full independence of ECB	• maintain full independence of ECB	• EcoFin to set inflation target for ECB	• suspend Stability and Growth Pact
• establish a free trade area with the US	• establish a free trade area with the US	• establish a free trade area with the US	• environment and labour standards in world trade	• environment and labour standards in world trade
• no EU-wide asylum or immigration policies	• EU 'blue card', to promote economic immigration	• liberal immigration, and full free movement of persons	• liberal immigration, and full free movement of persons	• liberal immigration, and full free movement of persons
• no EU foreign policy, defence policy via NATO	• EU foreign policies coordinated with US	• EU foreign policy to focus on use of 'soft power'	• EU foreign policy to focus on peace-keeping	• EU foreign policy based on peace and opposed to US

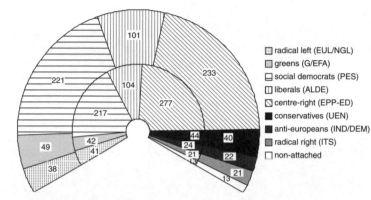

radical left (EUL/NGL)
greens (G/EFA)
social democrats (PES)
liberals (ALDE)
centre-right (EPP-ED)
conservatives (UEN)
anti-europeans (IND/DEM)
radical right (ITS)
non-attached

Figure 9.1 Make-up of the outgoing and incoming European Parliament, June 2009

As the results are announced gradually on Sunday evening, a slight shift leftwards in the new European Parliament becomes apparent, as figure 9.1 shows. The EPP remains the largest group, but they have lost some ground to the socialists, and the greens have gained several more seats. Analysis of the voting patterns by political scientists reveals that part of this shift can be explained by a mid-term swing away from centre-right governing parties in many member states, as is the usual case in European Parliament elections. However, analysis also reveals that the socialists and greens did disproportionately well in several member states because of the popularity and campaign efforts of Margot and Dany. On the other side, José was not so popular, as some citizens saw these elections as a chance to make a break with the past. Also, the liberal vote held up well in Central and Eastern Europe, as a result of Andrus's candidacy and vigorous campaign.

As head of the largest group in the European Parliament, the EPP group leader urges the governments to reappoint José for Commission President. However, it soon becomes clear that José does not command majority support in the new European

Parliament. Many of the liberal MEPs seem more likely to vote for Margot than José, given Margot's liberal policies on social and environmental issues and global trade. Dany concedes defeat and offers his support to Margot. The green and radical left MEPs immediately declare that they will support Margot.

José also does not command qualified-majority support (of 255 votes out of the 345) in the European Council. As table 9.2 shows, the European Council is split between Margot and José, with ten government leaders (with 150 votes) supporting Margot and ten (with 120 votes) supporting José. Of the remaining leaders, four support Bertie and three support Andrus. A deal will have to be done with these seven other leaders for Margot or José to secure sufficient support in the European Council.

Margot takes the initiative and calls a meeting with Andrus. She emphasises their joint commitment to protection of the environment, global free trade, a genuine single market in services, reducing the regulatory burden for small and medium-sized enterprises particularly in the service sector, liberal attitudes towards immigration and the full free movement of people inside the EU, and protection of employment rights of women and ethnic minorities and non-discrimination on the grounds of sexual orientation. She declares that she is willing to change her position on the Common Agricultural Policy, and to now support a re-nationalisation of part of the agricultural subsidies, and also that she will back Andrus's plan for a new carbon emissions trading system. She also promises to place liberals in some of the key portfolios in the Commission if she is elected as Commission President. In return for these commitments, Andrus declares his support for Margot, and encourages the liberal MEPs to do the same.

The deal between the socialists and liberals is finally sealed when the socialist group agrees to vote for the liberal candidate for president of the European Parliament in return for the

Table 9.2 Hypothetical line-up in the July 2009 European Council						
Member state	National party of PM or president	European party membership	Left–Right position of national party	QMV votes	Candidate supported in EP Election	Candidate voted for in European Council
Lithuania	LSDP	PES	0.30	7	Margot	Margot
Bulgaria	BSP	PES	0.32	10	Margot	Margot
Hungary	MSZP	PES	0.32	12	Margot	Margot
Denmark	SD	PES	0.35	7	Margot	Margot
Slovakia	Smer	PES	0.35	7	Margot	Margot
Spain	PSOE	PES	0.38	27	Margot	Margot
Portugal	PS	PES	0.40	12	Margot	Margot
Austria	SPO	PES	0.41	10	Margot	Margot
United Kingdom	Lab	PES	0.52	29	Margot	Margot
Italy	PD	EDP	0.37	29	Margot	Margot
Cyprus	DIKO	ELDR	0.51	4	Andrus	Margot
Romania	PNL	ELDR	0.58	14	Andrus	Margot
Finland	KESK	ELDR	0.58	7	Andrus	Margot
Estonia	Ref	ELDR	0.96	4	Andrus	Margot
Ireland	FF	AEN	0.65	7	Bertie	Margot
Poland	PiS	AEN	0.76	27	Bertie	Margot

				Bertie	Margot
Czech Republic	CDS	ED	12		Margot
Malta	PN	EPP	3	José	José
Belgium	CD&V	EPP	12	José	José
Luxembourg	CSV	EPP	4	José	José
Netherlands	CDA	EPP	13	José	José
Germany	CDU	EPP	29	José	José
France	LMP	EPP	29	José	José
Slovenia	SDS	EPP	4	José	José
Greece	ND	EPP	12	José	José
Sweden	M	EPP	10	José	Margot
Latvia	TP	EPP	4	José	José

For the member states that will not have an election before July 2009, I have assumed that the sitting prime minister or president (in the case of France and Cyprus) will still be in power in July 2009. For the nine member states where there will be an election before July 2009 – Malta (Spring 2008), Greece (Spring 2008), Spain (Spring 2008), Slovenia (Autumn 2008), Latvia (Autumn 2008), Romania (Autumn 2008), Denmark (Spring 2009), Portugal (Spring 2009) and Luxembourg (Summer 2009), I have guessed the electoral outcome from opinion poll standings of the main parties. The left–right location of the national parties are based on judgements by political scientists from each member state about the location of parties on a scale from 0 (most left) to 1 (most right), see Benoit and Laver (2006) and Marks (2007).

liberal group voting for Margot for Commission President. With the support of the socialists, liberals, greens and radical left MEPs, Margot now has a clear majority in the European Parliament. The pressure is now on the governments to support her candidacy in the European Council. The EPP try to block her and hold out for José. But, Margot holds meetings with the centre-right prime ministers who are not members of the EPP, in Poland, Ireland and the Czech Republic. She reassures each of them that she will govern from the centre rather than from the left, that she is not a Eurofederalist, and that she will allow national parliaments to review and potentially block all her legislative initiatives. After several decades of more integrationist Commission Presidents, these less federalist prime ministers are willing to give Margot a chance. The conservative prime minister of Sweden also announces that he will support her candidacy. Margot is still a few votes short of the 255 required for a qualified majority in the European Council, but her 235 votes are considerably more than José's 110.

The European Council meets at the end of June. Nine heads of government still support José. However, they agree not to block Margot because she commands a clear majority in the European Council. Margot is duly nominated by the heads of state and government without a formal vote taking place. She then wins a clear majority in the vote in the first plenary of the newly elected European Parliament in July. The vote is held by secret ballot, but it is clear that the socialist, liberal, green and radical left groups voted for her, as did some of the MEPs in the EPP and UEN groups.

The other members of the Commission are now nominated following the established practice: where each member state nominates a member of the Commission, and the Commission President has the power to veto any politician she does not want. The Estonian government nominates Andrus, who is granted the internal market portfolio. Margot requests that the

German government nominate Dany, who she would like for the environment portfolio, but the German coalition government refuses. Nevertheless, several other allies of Margot are placed in key positions, in the competition, industry, agriculture, trade, justice and interior affairs, and external relations portfolios. The Commission as a whole passes an investiture vote in the European Parliament in October and takes office in November 2009.

Margot presents the programme for the first few years of administration to the European Parliament in January 2010. It is an ambitious programme, which includes provisions to liberalise labour markets and social regulations for small and medium-sized enterprises, to fully implement the Services Directive, to reform the carbon emissions trading system, to reform the Common Agricultural Policy while increasing EU spending on research and development, and to liberalise economic migration into the EU and to implement the full free movement of person between the EU27 states. She also calls on the member states to give her authority to start negotiating a new global climate change package, to replace the Kyoto agreement. And, to improve coordination of fiscal policies by the governments and monetary policy by the European Central Bank, she proposes that the Economic and Finance Council should set an annual Eurozone inflation target for the European Central Bank.[2] The new EU agenda is set, and with a broad coalition in support of these policies in the European Parliament and the Council, there is a reasonable chance that the EU will be able to undertake some major policy reforms.

Finally, the more open contest, the media coverage of the debate between the candidates, and the changes in the way the European Parliament election campaigns were conducted, changed the way many citizens understand and see the EU. The Spring 2010 Eurobarometer opinion polls reveal that for the first time most European citizens know the name of their

Commission President. The polls also indicate that a majority of people have some idea of the policies the new Commission President has promised to pursue and that these policies are supported by a centre-left coalition at the European level. And, perhaps most importantly, the polls show that this policy agenda is supported by a majority of the public in most member states and a significant proportion of the public in the other member states. Democratic politics in the EU has finally arrived!

CHAPTER TEN

Conclusion and response to potential critiques

The European Union is a historic achievement. The new political and economic architecture in Europe guarantees the security and prosperity of almost half a billion people, generates social and economic opportunities and freedoms that were almost unthinkable a generation or two ago, and ensures that the rest of the world is no longer threatened by Europe's failure to resolve the historical rivalries between its peoples.

Nevertheless, the EU could be far more effective, legitimate and democratic. First, Europe faces several major policy challenges, such as service sector liberalisation, stable and sustainable energy, climate change, migration across and into Europe, and our relations with the US, our near neighbours, the developing world and the rising Asian powers. Each of these questions requires political leadership, political debates and political decisions, and will create political winners and losers, at least in the short term. If the EU continues to work primarily through independent regulators and consensual deals behind closed doors, the result will be policy gridlock and policy failure.

Second, there has been a dramatic decline in the popular legitimacy of the EU. Whereas in the early 1990s almost 75 per cent of people believed that their country's membership of the EU was 'a good thing', today the figure is only about 50 per cent. The decline in support for the EU has occurred across all member states and all social groups. It is true that many people take the benefits of the EU for granted. However, it is also true that the costs and benefits from European market integration, economic and monetary union and enlargement from fifteen to twenty-seven states are gradually becoming clear. While social and economic elites have benefited, the benefits to lower-skilled and lower-paid sections of society, particularly in some of the founding states in Western Europe, are less clear. Furthermore, an increasing number of people disagree with the types of policies coming from the EU. Voters on the left oppose the downward pressures on public spending, corporate tax rates and wages that result from market integration and liberalisation. Meanwhile, voters on the right oppose new social and environmental costs on businesses, liberal migration policies and new rights for ethnic minorities and homosexuals.

Third, as new powers have been passed to the EU, concerns about a 'democratic deficit' have arisen. The checks-and-balances in the institutional design of the EU ensure that most European level policies are moderate. But, producing policies that are close to the views of a notional average European citizen without there ever being a political debate and a political choice about these policies means that the EU is not really a democratic polity. Democracy means competition for political office and over the direction of the policy agenda, yet in the EU no such competition exists. National elections are about national governments and national policies, despite the fact that almost 50 per cent of what European governments now do is in Brussels. European Parliament elections are also not about Europe, as they are little more than mid-term contests in national electoral cycles.

Facing these problems, it was no surprise that the French and Dutch citizens rejected the EU Constitution. Domestic issues certainly played a role in these votes, but the evidence suggests that in both cases concerns about the ineffectiveness, unaccountability and undesirability of the EU and its policies were the dominant factors. And, had the Constitution not been rejected in these two countries it almost certainly would have been rejected in several of the other states that were due to hold referendums. Clearly something is very wrong when such an important political and economic achievement as the European Union is so unpopular with so many people in so many countries.

Four main views have been put forward by commentators and decision-makers about how to get out of the current crisis. Yet none of these positions would resolve the current problems.

One view is that the EU should *do nothing*: 'if it ain't broke, don't fix it'.[1] The argument here is that the EU is designed to do a specific and limited set of things, such as the creation and regulation of the internal market, and the EU does these things quite well. Further institutional reform or political change in the way the EU works, so the argument goes, is a distraction and will inevitably provoke conflict because the EU cannot and should not be a more political union. The EU just needs to be given more time, to complete the internal market, to make economic and monetary union work, and to incorporate the twelve new member states.

I am sympathetic to parts of this argument. The EU is not and should not be a 'federal superstate'. I also agree that further treaty reforms are a distraction, as the basic political architecture of the EU is already close to equilibrium. However, this argument underestimates the extent of the current crisis. The policy agenda of the EU has shifted, away from market-creating to what policies should be pursued in the new continental-scale polity. Faced with the new policy challenges, isolating EU decision-making from real political debates and choices will leave the EU gridlocked and further undermine the legitimacy of the project.

A second view is that the EU should *focus on public relations*. This view is most popular in parts of the Commission. The argument here is that citizens do not realise how much they benefit from the EU. If people were more informed about the benefits of the internal market and the other policies of the EU and learned more about how the EU works, they would inevitably start to love it!

It is certainly true that many citizens do not know much about the EU and take for granted the benefits of economic and political integration in Europe. However, there is little evidence that providing citizens with more information about the EU and its policies would increase popular support for the project. Opinion polls reveal that public understanding about the EU has increased over the last decade at the same time that public support has declined. For those already opposed to the EU, providing more information about the EU is easily dismissed as 'propaganda'. More significantly, as people learn more about the EU they start to understand that economic integration benefits some social groups more than others, that they pay significant amounts into the EU budget yet find it difficult to identify what they receive in return, and that it is almost impossible for them to change the direction of EU policies.

A third view is that the EU should *focus on procedural reforms*, such as the revised version of the Constitution, the Lisbon Treaty, that was agreed by the EU governments in October 2007. This is the position of most of the pro-Constitution governments, such as the German chancellor, Angela Merkel. The argument here is that reforming the institutions will give a new impetus to European integration, bring the EU closer to the citizens and make the institutions more effective.

There is little evidence for this position. The Constitution or even the slimmed down version of it in the Lisbon Treaty would not change the basic policy and institutional architecture of the EU much. The Constitution was largely a symbolic exercise in the first place. And once the constitutional symbols – such as the name of the document, the mention of the EU flag and anthem, and the title 'EU Foreign Minister' – have been stripped from the document, what remains is probably the least significant treaty the EU has ever signed. Unlike all previous treaties, the 'Lisbon Treaty' would neither allocate any significant new policy competences to the EU nor alter the balance of powers between the EU institutions (by strengthening the power of the Commission or the European Parliament). For example, a single President of the European Council, as proposed in the Lisbon Treaty, may be more effective than the current rotating Presidency of the Council. However, the European Council president would be largely a ceremonial post as the dominant office in the EU would still be the Commission President, since the Commission would still control all the powers of legislative initiative.

Furthermore, the new treaty reforms are unlikely to bring the EU closer to the citizens, and may even undermine the legitimacy of the EU further if a second attempt to ratify a new treaty is rejected. And, even if the new treaty is ratified and eventually enters into force, the minor institutional changes are not significant enough to enable the EU to overcome policy gridlock or make the EU more democratically accountable. These problems can only be addressed if the political elites change the way they behave within the institutional set-up of the EU.

A fourth view is that the EU should *focus on policy delivery*. This is the view of the British government and José Barroso, the Commission President. The argument here is that the EU is failing to deliver the policies that citizens want. The EU should hence focus on reforming unpopular policies (such as the common agricultural policy and certain business regulations), promoting popular policies (such as environmental protection), and reforming the economy (by liberalising services and labour markets). The economy would then pick up and citizens would start to appreciate the good things that Brussels does.

There are two problems with this argument. First, unless the problem of policy gridlock can be overcome the EU has almost no chance of delivering any of these policies. Second, even if these policies could be delivered, there would be widespread opposition to many of them unless a democratic mandate could be achieved. Unlike the creation of the internal market, these new policies would have significant redistributive outcomes: less money for small farmers, new environmental costs for businesses, greater competition for domestic service providers, and job insecurity for semi-skilled workers. These 'policy losers' would no doubt become even more anti-European than they currently are.

My solution to the current problems facing the EU is consequently rather different. Europe's leaders should focus, I believe, on gradually promoting 'limited democratic politics' at the European level. This has already started. As a result of the major treaty reforms of the 1980s and 1990s, a political coalition already has the potential to agree a policy agenda and build alliances to pass this agenda through the Commission, the Council and the European Parliament. Furthermore, inside the institutions, coalitions have started to be built along political lines. This is most advanced in the European Parliament, where the political groups play a powerful role, but is also developing in the Council as well as in the relations between the Commission and the other two institutions. This is significant, as it means that battles in the EU policy process will divide and unite people along lines that cut across national boundaries. Such cross-territorial politics was essential for the development of democratic identities at the national level in Europe and will be essential if there is ever going to be a genuine democratic identification with the EU (a *demos*).

However, if this emerging politics in Brussels is to lead to policy reform and greater EU accountability, our elected politicians must compete and form cross-institutional alliances at the European level in a more transparent fashion. More open contestation and coalition-building would increase the stakes, which in turn would encourage policy innovation and reward success and punish failure. More open contestation and coalition-building would also encourage the media to cover the Brussels soap opera for the first time, which would lead to greater public identification of those who 'govern' at the European level.

The EU does not need further treaty reforms to encourage 'limited democratic politics'. What is needed is for the politicians at the EU level to compete and coalesce in a far more political and transparent fashion. The most effective way of promoting this is to change some of the informal practices and procedures of the EU institutions. Box 10.1 summarises the changes I proposed in chapter 8. National parties, the media and citizens would treat European Parliament elections more seriously if a majority coalition in the European Parliament was able to elect the president of the European Parliament and control most of the key policy-making positions (such as committee chairs). Interest groups and citizens would be able to see what coalitions formed between governments if the Council worked more like a normal legislature, with full access to amendments and full coverage of discussions, decisions and votes. And, there would be a more accountable connection between policy commitments and outcomes if there was a more open contest for the Commission President.

Encouraging the gradual development of limited democratic politics in the EU is far better than the other options on the table. It is relatively low risk precisely because it would be 'limited' by the checks-and-balances of the EU system, which ensure that very broad coalitions would have to be built on each issue and the losers on one issue would most likely be on the winning side on other issues. For example, while a social democrat, liberal and green coalition might win on social and

Box 10.1 How to encourage limited democratic politics in the EU

European Parliament: *A winner-takes-more model*

- Elect the president of the European Parliament for a five-year term rather than a two-and-a-half-year term

- Replace the purely proportional system for allocating committee chairs with a system which gives the larger political groups more chairs (either via a 'winners' bonus model' or a 'modified d'Hondt model')

EU Council: *A proper and transparent legislature*

- Make all legislative documents in the Council publicly available, including meeting agendas, proposals, amendments, verbatim reports of proceedings, and full and complete minutes

- Open all legislative deliberation in the Council to the public

- Restrict the right to propose legislative amendments to coalitions of governments – e.g. an amendment must be supported by at least 14% of governments (4 out of the current 27) who together command at least 14% of the Council votes (49 out of the current 345)

- Put all legislative decisions in the Council to a vote, and record the outcomes in the minutes

European Commission: *An open contest for the Commission President*

- Allow rival candidates for the Commission President to be proposed by groups of national party leaders before European Parliament elections

- Make the candidates set out their policy agenda ('manifesto') for their five-year term

- Hold a live public debate between the candidates in the European Parliament

- Allow the manifesto commitments of the winner to guide the allocation of Commission portfolios and a multi-annual work programme of the Commission

environmental reforms, a coalition of liberals, conservatives and moderate social democrats might win on market liberalisation issues.

There are also high potential benefits of limited democratic politics in the EU. There would be greater policy competition and the emergence of a mandate for policy change. Citizens would be able to see the governing alliances at the European level, to gradually accept being on the losing side in one period or on some issues in return for being on the winning side in some future period or on other issues. And, the EU would gradually evolve from the current semi-despotic system into a partially democratic system, and in time a fully democratic system might emerge in response to citizens' demands.

There are numerous potential criticisms of my ideas. As a pre-emptive strike, here are some responses to some of them.

One of the main potential criticisms is that politicising the EU would fundamentally change its nature, since the 'community method' would be replaced by partisan politics. The community method, used in this way, refers to the Commission as a non-political actor and consensus decision-making between the governments. Some people believe that politicising the EU would turn the Commission into a 'political executive' and turn the Council into a 'political legislature', which is not what the EU's founding fathers intended.

I agree! In other words, the EU would no longer work the way the founding fathers intended. However, the old community method is already dead. The EU of 27 today is a very different animal to the EU of 6, 12 or 15. What the EU needed while the internal market and the institutions were being built was a non-political Commission and a largely consensual Council. The situation today is very different. Either policymakers should accept that the EU now makes fundamentally political decisions, which constrain the democratic choices of citizens and produce winners and losers, and so should allow the EU to be politicised, or they may have to accept that the EU will gradually wither away as larger and larger numbers of citizens turn against it.

A second criticism, which is related to the first one, is that limited democratic politics may undermine EU legitimacy even further. This claim is based on the idea that democratic competition will produce winners and losers and those citizens and parties who find themselves on the losing side would not accept the winning coalition as legitimate.

In response I would point out that the losers from the current policies of the EU and the likely policy reforms are already pretty clear. More transparent coalitions would allow those on the losing side on some issues to recognise that they are on the winning side on other issues and also have a chance of being on the winning side on the issues they currently lose on at some point in the future. So, instead of the French left rejecting the EU for being a neo-liberal project, they would recognise that the current policies on market deregulation are a result of the current centre-right majorities in the Commission, Council and European Parliament. A liberal–social democratic coalition actually wins on most environmental issues and many social issues, and the governing coalition on market reform issues could be very different in the not too distant future.

A third critique is that my cure for the EU is too similar to the Westminster model of government. All I am doing, so I have heard some people claim, is presenting a typically narrow British perspective to Europe.

At one level, this criticism is rather insulting, as my views are based on research and analysis as a political scientist and have very little to do with my nationality. Many German, Belgian, Italian, Dutch, Spanish and Scandinavian political scientists hold similar views to mine. At another level, this criticism is simply wrong. Limited democratic politics in the EU would be nothing like politics in Westminster. Whereas in Britain an electoral plurality can dominate policy outcomes, governing majorities at the European level inevitably have to be 'supersized', more like Belgium, Scandinavia, Switzerland or Germany.

A fourth criticism is that it would be impossible to isolate 'constitutional politics', about the design of the EU, from 'normal politics', about social and economic policies.[2] From this perspective, politicising the EU would be dangerous as there would be new battles about whether certain policies should be passed back to the national level, whether the balance of power between the institutions should be changed, and which countries should join or even remain as members of the EU.

In response, the basic constitutional structure of the EU has been politicised for some time, in highly contested referendums, parliamentary votes and constitutional court rulings in almost all member states. Above all, though, I do not see why constitutional politics and so-called normal politics should be separated. If there is going to be any change to the current institutional equilibrium, this should emerge through democratic debate and contestation, as it has done at the national level in Belgium, Spain, Italy, the UK and many other territorially divided polities. For example, a contest for the Commission President would probably lead to the candidates taking different positions on enlargement and budgetary reform, which are semi-constitutional matters in the EU. This would not undermine the whole EU system and may in fact produce more legitimate outcomes on these and related issues.

A fifth criticism is that left–right politics at the European and national levels are quite different, and so European parties would not be able to articulate and cohere around clear policy positions in a more politicised EU. For example, on the issue of economic reform, the French right (such as Nicolas Sarkozy) tend to be on the left at the European level while the British left (such as Gordon Brown) tend to be on the right!

In response, it is certainly true that positions and alignments at the national and European levels do not always coincide. However, this is not a problem. What will probably happen if limited democratic politics develops in the EU is that a new structure of European parties would emerge as new coalitions and alignments replace the old ones. This would be like the evolution of party systems at the national level in Europe after universal suffrage in the early twentieth century, where the old parliamentary parties were replaced by completely new parties and coalitions.

Sixth, even if some people agree with my diagnosis of the problems and are sympathetic to my suggested solutions, a common criticism is that limited democratic politics cannot develop in the EU unless there is further treaty reform. For example, if the European Parliament was granted more power, such as the ability to amend all areas of the budget, there would be more at stake in European Parliament elections. If QMV was extended to all policy areas, such as taxation, there would be more open battles in the Council. And, if the Commission President were nominated by the European Parliament rather than the European Council, the parties in the European Parliament would present rival candidates for the post in European Parliament elections.

These institutional reforms would certainly promote more political contestation in the EU. However, I am sceptical that the twenty-seven governments would ever agree to such reforms, none of which were in the draft EU Constitution or are in the current Lisbon Treaty. And, even if the governments could agree, such dramatic reforms would almost certainly be rejected by several member states. Also, I am not convinced that such reforms are a good idea, as they would get rid of some of the checks-and-balances in the EU system, and so would increase the risk of gradually politicising the EU.

Above all, though, I believe that politics is the product of both institutional design and political behaviour. Constitutional rules certainly set the limits of what is politically feasible, but within these limits there is always plenty of room for manoeuvre. For example, under the nineteenth-century constitutions, parliaments across Europe gradually took over control of the executive from monarchs. Similarly, within the limits set by the current EU treaties, the elites could change the way politics works quite dramatically, to allow more competition, debate and coalition-formation.

A seventh criticism is that if the solution is so obvious, why have the elites not already done it? Clearly, the governments, the parties in the European Parliament, and the Commission have not allowed more open democratic politics because at least some of them do not want it. And, if these actors do not want it, then there is no chance of it happening!

I find this critique the hardest to refute. Several key actors are clearly opposed to politicising the EU. The Council has not been fully opened up because some governments fear that their publics would see them losing on some key issues. The European Parliament has not become a more majoritarian institution because the parties that expect to be in the minority under such a system have resisted any such move. And, some commissioners fear that their legitimacy would be undermined if they become a more explicitly political body.

However, there are reasons to be optimistic. The governments who are in favour of reforming EU policies have a lot to gain from limited democratic politics, as they have very little hope of their policy objectives being achieved without it. The liberal group in the European Parliament, which is likely to be pivotal in the formation of a majority coalition, would almost certainly gain more influence if policy-making powers in the chamber were allocated in a more majoritarian way. The two largest groups in the European Parliament, the EPP and the socialists, together with the liberals have easily enough votes to change the parliament's rules of the procedure in the ways I have suggested. And, there is growing frustration in the Commission about policy gridlock and declining public support for the EU. If the regulatory and political functions of the Commission could be separated – by delegating regulatory functions to independent regulators, such as a European Cartel Office – the Commission would benefit enormously from more open democratic politics in the EU.

Ultimately, Europe's elites will only allow the EU to become more politicised if they recognise that the EU faces a crisis and believe that this is the best way out of the crisis. Following the referendums in France and the Netherlands, some political leaders in Europe recognise the problems and are trying to think about how to address them. However, many others are still living in cloud cuckoo land! The time is right for social scientists, policy-makers, journalists, interest groups, NGOs and private citizens to convince our leaders that the EU is in trouble and that a more openly political and democratic Europe is the best solution.

Notes

CHAPTER 2 WHY THE EUROPEAN UNION IS MORE
NECESSARY THAN EVER

1 The idea of a tension between economic and political logics in the
formation and collapse of polities is common in the study of
history as well as more formal political economy analysis. See, for
example, Lieven's (2000) work on empire, and Alesina's and
Spolaore's (2003) work on the size of nations.

2 The benefits of economic size go back to Adam Smith's argument
that specialisation of labour is limited by the size of the market.
The most extensive recent work on the relationship between
economic performance and the size of countries is Alesina and
Spolaore (2003), which makes the case that larger economies are
generally better than smaller economies. Also see Robinson
(1960). However, the benefits of a large economy relative to a
small economy are not universally accepted by economists. See,
for example, Rose (2006).

3 For example, Alesina and Spolaore (2003) find that smaller states
not only need an open world trading system to prosper but also
need more government spending per capita than larger states, to
provide basic public goods and to sustain high levels of
comparative productivity. Peter Katzenstein (1985) makes a similar
argument about the economic success of small European states,
which he attributed to their openness to the global economy plus
their corporatist and coordinated economic models.

4 Olson (1982) also argues that small homogenous societies are
less likely to suffer from collective action problems.

5 See Almond (1956) and Lipset (1960).

6 As a Ph.D. student of Almond, Arend Lijphart rejected his
mentor's idea that democratic government was only possible in

homogeneous societies or societies with cross-cutting cleavages. However, Lijphart's solution, of rules that force elites to cooperate rather than compete, accepts that democracy is necessarily heavily constrained in deeply divided societies. See, for example, Lijphart (1968, 1977).

7 This was a headline figure in the Cecchini Report on 'The Cost of Non-Europe' (Cecchini et al., 1988).

8 See http://ec.europa.eu/internal_market/top_layer/benefits_en.htm (accessed on 20 April 2007).

9 OECD data, see http://www.oecd.org/dataoecd/14/3/8264806.xls (accessed on 20 April 2007).

10 See Katzenstein (1985).

11 See, in particular, Eichengreen (2007), pp. 18–19.

12 Tradable sectors are those sectors that could conceivably be located anywhere, such as most manufacturing sectors and some service sectors. Non-tradable sectors, in contrast, are those parts of the economy that cannot be easily relocated, such as most of the public sector (for example, healthcare and education provision) and many local services (for example, tourism, catering, building, plumbing, etc.). On the effects of market integration on tradable and non-tradable sectors see, for example, Frieden (1991).

13 This 'cloture rule' in the US Senate was introduced in 1917. For the effect of the checks-and-balances and supermajority rules on policy-making in the US, which equally apply to the EU, see Krehbiel (1998).

14 This description is similar to Sapir's (2006) analysis. Esping-Andersen's (1990) 'three worlds of welfare capitalism' broadly fits with the first three models identified here.

15 Parliamentary systems, particularly with proportional electoral systems and coalition governments, generally have higher levels of public spending than presidential systems, because a separation of power between the executive and the legislature in presidential systems tends to prevent policy change, such as increases in public spending from a low base. See, in particular, Tsebelis (2002), and Persson and Tabellini (2003). Alesina and Glaeser (2004) also point to the effect of geographic and social diversity in Europe compared to America, where a larger geographic area and a more heterogeneous society in America has reduced the extent of

economic redistribution possible compared to most European
countries.

16 See, for example, Donohue and Pollack (2001).

CHAPTER 3 POLICY GRIDLOCK

1 For a more thorough and sophisticated analysis of the need for
economic reform in Europe see Alesina and Giavazzi (2006).

2 See, especially, Lijphart (1999) and Tsebelis (2002).

3 Strictly speaking, the Nice Treaty, which entered into force in
2003, made Council decision-making slightly more difficult, by
increased the QMV threshold to 73.9 per cent from 71.3 per cent
and by adding the two additional criteria, relating to the majority
of member states and 62 per cent of total EU population.

4 This quote is allegedly attributed to Austin Mitchell, who has
been the Labour MP for Grimsby since 1977.

5 See, for example, Tsebelis, Jensen, Kalandrakis and Kreppel
(2001) and Kreppel (2002).

6 See Hix (2002).

7 The distinction I make between market creation and policy
reform is similar, although not identical, to the distinction
between 'negative' and 'positive' integration; where 'negative
integration' refers to the removal of existing national rules (for
example, in the creation of the single market) and 'positive
integration' refers to the adoption of new common rules (for
example, in social and environmental policy) (cf. Scharpf, 1999).
I should thank Ben Crum for pointing this out.

8 The Services Directive was actually proposed by Fritz Bolkestein
in the Prodi Commission, but the Barroso Commission came out
strongly in support of the proposal.

9 Hans-Gert Poettering of the German CDU was leader of the EPP
and Martin Schulz of the German SPD was leader of the PES.

CHAPTER 4 LACK OF POPULAR LEGITIMACY

1 See Glencross and Trechsel (2007).

2 See Franklin and Wlezien (1997) for example.

3 These percentages exclude the 'don't knows'.

4 See, in particular, Eichenberg and Dalton (1993).
5 See Franklin, Marsh and McLaren (1994).
6 See the Presidency Conclusions of the European Council Meeting in Laeken, 14 and 15 December 2001, p. 20.
7 See Easton (1965, 1975).
8 See, in particular, Gabel (1998), pp. 2–35.
9 Cf. Anderson and Reichert (1996).

CHAPTER 5 A DEMOCRATIC DEFICIT

1 Rohrschneider (2002).
2 For an earlier attempt to identify a 'standard version' of the democratic deficit see Weiler et al. (1995).
3 Many of the arguments in this chapter are outlined in more detail in Føllesdal and Hix (2006).
4 See, for example, Andersen and Burns (1996) and Raunio (1999).
5 See, for example, Williams (1991) and Lodge (1994).
6 In particular, Scharpf (1997, 1999).
7 This argument is most powerfully made by Streeck and Schmitter (1991).
8 See Moravcsik (2002, 2003).
9 For example, see the European Commission's PreLex service (http://ec.europa.eu/prelex/apcnet.cfm?CL=en), and the European Parliament's Legislative Observatory (http://www.europarl.europa.eu/oeil/index.jsp?language=en).
10 Moravcsik (2002), p. 605.
11 For example, these are the measures used by organisations such as Freedom House (http://www.freedomhouse.org) and projects like 'Polity IV' (http://www.cidcm.umd.edu/polity) to decide whether a country is democratic.
12 See Schumpeter (1943).
13 Schattschneider (1960), p. 141.
14 Especially Dahl (1971). Also see Przeworski et al. (2000).
15 See the research of the Party Manifestos research group, Klingemann et al. (2006).
16 See, in particular, Hug (2002).
17 Hallstein (1972), p. 74.
18 Reif and Schmitt (1980).
19 See, for example, Hix and Marsh (2007).

20 Minder and Parker (2004).
21 For a comprehensive assessment which focuses mainly on these
    procedural aspects of democratic accountability in the EU see
    Lord (2004).
22 See, in particular, Crombez (2003).

CHAPTER 6 THE CASE FOR 'LIMITED DEMOCRATIC POLITICS' IN THE EU

1 See, in particular, Majone (1996).
2 See, for example, Dehousse (1995), Majone (2002) and Moravcsik
   (2002).
3 For example, Frieden and Rogowski (1996).
4 Cf. Pierson and Leibfried (1995).
5 See, in particular, Anderson et al. (2005).
6 See, for example, Weiler (1995).
7 See, in particular, Rokkan (1999).
8 Key (1961).

CHAPTER 7 HOW THE EU IS READY FOR LIMITED DEMOCRATIC POLITICS

1 See, in particular, Powell (2000) on how governments in
   consensual/proportional systems, such as Scandinavia or the
   Benelux, are more likely to contain the party which the average
   voter supports than governments in majoritarian systems, such
   as the United Kingdom.
2 See, in particular, Hix, Noury and Roland (2007).
3 The method is known as NOMINATE, and was developed by
   Poole and Rosenthal for the study of voting in the US Congress.
   See Poole and Rosenthal (1997).
4 See, in particular, the analysis in Hix and Noury (2007), where we
   demonstrate that the left-right location of an MEP is a strong
   predictor of how he or she votes in the European Parliament on
   migration issues.
5 See Hix, Noury and Roland (2005).
6 See, for example, Golub (1999).
7 Mattila and Lane (2001).

8 See Mattila (2004).
9 See Mattila (2004), Hagemann (2006), Hayes-Renshaw, Van Aken and Wallace (2006) and Hagemann and De Clerck-Sachsse (2007); cf. Zimmer, Schneider and Dobbins (2005).
10 Hagemann and De Clerck-Sachsse (2007).
11 In a sense, Jacques Delors is the exception that proves the general rule that under unanimity the Commission president was inevitably a moderate politician. Delors was in fact chosen as a compromise candidate after Margaret Thatcher had threatened to veto Claude Cheysson, who she regarded as too 'federalist'. Only later did it become clear that Delors was a far more dynamic and confrontational politician than Thatcher had expected.
12 See Benoit and Laver (2006) and Marks (2007). I have rescaled the Benoit and Laver and Marks scales from 0 to 1 for convenience.
13 See Hix, Noury and Roland (2007), ch. 10.
14 See Hix and Lord (1996) and Gabel and Hix (2002).
15 European Parliament (1999), p. 137.

CHAPTER 8 ENCOURAGING DEMOCRATIC POLITICS IN THE EU

1 See, for example, Corbett et al. (2007).
2 See http://ec.europa.eu/prelex/apcnet.cfm?CL=en.
3 Hayes-Renshaw, Van Aken and Wallace (2006).
4 Official Journal of the European Communities, Debates of the European Parliament, 21 July 1994, p. 66.

CHAPTER 9 A SCENARIO: THE 2009 EUROPEAN COMMISSION PRESIDENT CONTEST

1 These are hypothetical candidates. Any connection with actual politicians is purely coincidental!
2 This is similar to the British model, where the chancellor of the exchequer sets the inflation target and the Monetary Policy Committee of the Bank of England sets interest rates.

CHAPTER 10 CONCLUSION AND RESPONSE TO
POTENTIAL CRITIQUES

1 Moravcsik (2003).
2 See, in particular, Bartolini (2006).

References

Alesina, Alberto and Francesco Giavazzi (2006) *The Future of Europe: Reform or Decline*. Cambridge, MA: Massachusetts Institute of Technology Press.

Alesina, Alberto and Edward L. Glaeser (2004) *Fighting Poverty in the US and Europe: A World of Difference*. Oxford: Oxford University Press.

Alesina, Alberto and Enrico Spolaore (2003) *The Size of Nations*. Cambridge, MA: Massachusetts Institute of Technology Press.

Almond, Gabriel (1956) 'Comparative political systems', *Journal of Politics* 18(3): 391–409.

Anderson, Christopher J. and M. Shawn Reichert (1996) 'Economic benefits and support for membership in the E.U.: a cross-national analysis', *Journal of Public Policy* 15(3): 231–49.

Anderson, Christopher J., André Blais, Shaun Bowler, Todd Donovan and Ola Listhaug (2005) *Losers' Consent: Elections and Democratic Legitimacy*, Oxford: Oxford University Press.

Andersen, Svein S. and Tom Burns (1996) 'The European Union and the erosion of parliamentary democracy: a study of post-parliamentary governance'. In Svein S. Andersen and Kjell A. Eliassen (eds) *The European Union: How Democratic Is It?* London: Sage.

Bartolini, Stefano (2006) 'Should the Union Be "politicised"? Prospects and risks'. In Stefano Bartolini and Simon Hix (2006) *Politics: The Right or the Wrong Sort of Medicine for the EU?*, Policy Paper No. 19, Notre Europe.

Benoit, Kenneth and Michael Laver (2006) *Party Policy in Modern Democracies*. London: Routledge.

Bräuninger, Thomas and Thomas König (2001) Indices of Power IOP 2.0 [computer program]. Konstanz: University of Konstanz. [http://www.uni-konstanz.de/FuF/Verwiss/Köenig /IOP.html].

Cecchini, Paolo, et al. (1988) *The European Challenge, 1992: The Benefits of a Single Market*. Aldershot: Gower.

Corbett, Richard, Francis Jacobs and Michael Shackleton (2007) *The European Parliament*, 7th edition. London: John Harper Publishing.

Cowgill, Anthony and Andrew Cowgill (2004) *The European Constitution in Perspective: Analysis and Review of 'The Treaty Establishing A Constitution for Europe'*. Stroud: British Management Data Foundation.

Crombez, Christophe (2003) 'The democratic deficit in the European Union: much ado about nothing', *European Union Politics* 4(1): 101–20.

Dahl, Robert A. (1971) *Polyarchy: Participation and Opposition*. New Haven, CT: Yale University Press.

Dehousse, Renaud (1995) 'Constitutional reform in the European Community: are there alternatives to the majoritarian avenue?' In Jack Hayward (ed.) *The Crisis of Representation in Europe*. London: Frank Cass.

Donohue, John D. and Mark A. Pollack (2001) 'Centralization and its Discontents: the rhythms of federalism in the United States and the European Union'. In Kalypso Nicolaïdis and Robert Howse (eds) *The Federal Vision: Legitimacy and Levels of Governance in the United States and the European Union*. Oxford: Oxford University Press.

Easton, David (1965) *A Framework for Political Analysis*. Englewood Cliffs, NJ: Prentice Hall.

Easton, David (1975) 'A reassessment of the concept of political support', *British Journal of Political Science* 5: 435–57.

Eichenberg, Richard C. and Russell J. Dalton (1993) 'Europeans and the European Community: the dynamics of public support for European integration', *International Organization* 47(4): 507–34.

Eichengreen, Barry (2007) *The European Economy since 1945: Coordinated Capitalism and Beyond*. Princeton, NJ: Princeton University Press.

Esping-Andersen, Gøsta (1990) *The Three Worlds of Welfare Capitalism*. Princeton, NJ: Princeton University Press.

European Parliament (1999) *The Committee of Experts' Report on Fraud, Mismanagement and Nepotism in the European Commission*. Brussels: European Parliament.

Felsenthal, Dan S. and Moshé Machover (2001) 'The Treaty of Nice and qualified majority voting', *Social Choice and Welfare* 18(3): 431–64.

Føllesdal, Andreas and Simon Hix (2006) 'Why there is a democratic deficit in the EU: a response to Majone and Moravcsik', *Journal of Common Market Studies* 44(3): 533–62.

Franklin, Mark and Christopher Wlezien (1997) 'The responsive public: issue salience, policy change, and preferences for European Unification', *Journal of Theoretical Politics* 9(3): 347–63.

Franklin, Mark, Michael Marsh and Lauren McLaren (1994) 'Uncorking the bottle: popular opposition to European unification in the wake of Maastricht', *Journal of Common Market Studies* 32(4): 101–17.

Frieden, Jeffrey A. (1991) 'Invested interests: the politics of national economic policies in a world of global finance', *International Organization* 45(4): 425–51.

Frieden, Jeffrey A. and Ronald Rogowski (1996) 'The impact of the international political economy on national policies: an overview'. In Robert O. Keohane and Helen V. Milner (eds) *Internationalization and Domestic Politics*. Cambridge: Cambridge University Press.

Gabel, Matthew J. (1998) *Interests and Integration: Market Liberalization, Public Opinion, and European Union*. Ann Arbor, MI: University of Michigan Press.

Gabel, Matthew J. and Simon Hix (2002) 'The European Parliament and executive politics in the EU: voting behaviour and the Commission president investiture procedure'. In Madeleine Hosli, Adrian Van Deemen and Mika Widgrén (eds) *Institutional Challenges in the European Union*. London: Routledge.

Glencross, Andrew and Alexander H. Trechsel (2007) 'First or second order referendums? Understanding the votes on the Constitutional Treaty in four EU member states', manuscript, European University Institute.

Golub, Jonathan (1999) 'In the shadow of the vote? Decision making in the European Community', *International Organization* 53(4): 733–64.

Gwartney, James D., Robert Lawson and William Easterly (2006) *Economic Freedom of the World: 2006 Annual Report*. Vancouver, BC: The Fraser Institute.

Hagemann, Sara (2006) *Decision-Making in the European Union's Council of Ministers*, Ph.D. thesis. London: London School of Economics and Political Science.

Hagemann, Sara and Julia De Clerck-Sachsse (2007) *Old Rules, New Game: Decision-Making in the Council of Ministers after the 2004 Enlargement*. Brussels: Centre for European Policy Studies.

Hallstein, Walter (1972) *Europe in the Making*. London: Allen and Unwin.

Hayes-Renshaw, Fiona, Wim Van Aken and Helen Wallace (2006) 'When and why the EU Council of Ministers votes explicitly', *Journal of Common Market Studies* 44(1): 161–94.

Hix, Simon (2002) 'Constitutional agenda-setting through discretion in rule interpretation: why the European Parliament won at Amsterdam', *British Journal of Political Science* 32(2): 259–80.

Hix, Simon and Christopher Lord (1996) 'The making of a president: the European Parliament and the confirmation of Jacques Santer as president of the Commission', *Government and Opposition* 31(1): 62–76.

Hix, Simon and Michael Marsh (2007) 'Punishment or protest? Understanding European Parliament elections', *Journal of Politics* 69(2): 495–510.

Hix, Simon and Abdul Noury (2006) 'After enlargement: voting patterns in the sixth European Parliament', manuscript. London School of Economics and Political Science.

Hix, Simon and Abdul Noury (2007) 'Politics not economic interests: determinants of migration policies in the European Union', *International Migration Review* 41(1): 182–205.

Hix, Simon, Abdul Noury and Gérard Roland (2005) 'Power to the parties: cohesion and competition in the European Parliament, 1979–2001', *British Journal of Political Science* 35(2): 209–34.

Hix, Simon, Abdul Noury and Gérard Roland (2007) *Democratic Politics in the European Parliament*. Cambridge. Cambridge University Press.

Hug, Simon (2002) *Voices of Europe: Citizens, Referendums, and European Integration*. Lanham, MD: Rowman and Littlefield.

Katzenstein, Peter J. (1985) *Small States in World Markets: Industrial Policy in Europe*. Cornell, NY: Cornell University Press.

Key, Valdimer Orlando (1961) *Public Opinion and American Democracy*. New York: Knopf.

Klingemann, Hans-Dieter, Andrea Volkens, Judith Bara, Ian Budge and Michael D. McDonald (2006) *Mapping Policy Preferences II: Estimates for Parties, Electors, and Governments in Eastern Europe, European Union, and OECD 1990–2003.* Oxford: Oxford University Press.

König, Thomas, Brooke Luetgert and Tanja Dannwolf (2006) 'Quantifying European legislative research: using CELEX and PreLex in EU legislative studies', *European Union Politics* 7(4): 555–76.

Krehbiel, Keith (1998) *Pivotal Politics: A Theory of U.S. Lawmaking.* Chicago: Il: University of Chicago Press.

Kreppel, Amie (2002) 'Moving beyond procedure: an empirical analysis of European Parliament legislative influence', *Comparative Political Studies* 35(7): 784–813.

Lieven, Dominic (2000) *Empire: The Russian Empire and its Rivals.* London: John Murray.

Lijphart, Arend (1968) *The Politics of Accommodation: Pluralism and Democracy in the Netherlands.* Berkeley, CA: University of California Press.

Lijphart, Arend (1977) *Democracy in Plural Societies: A Comparative Exploration.* New Haven, CT: Yale University Press.

Lijphart, Arend (1999) *Patterns of Democracy: Government Forms and Performance in Thirty-Six Countries.* New Haven, CT: Yale University Press.

Lipset, Seymour Martin (1960) *Political Man: The Social Bases of Politics.* Garden City, NY: Doubleday & Co.

Lodge, Juliet (1994) 'The European Parliament and the authority-democracy crisis', *Annals of the American Academy of Political and Social Science* 531: 69–83.

Lord, Christopher (2004) *A Democratic Audit of the European Union.* Basingstoke: Palgrave.

Maddison, Angus (2006) *Historical Statistics for the World Economy: 1–2003 AD.* http://www.ggdc.net/maddison.

Majone, Giandomenico (1996) *Regulating Europe.* London: Routledge.

Majone, Giandomenico (2002) 'The European Commission: the limits of centralization and the perils of parliamentarization', *Governance* 15(3): 375–92.

Marks, Gary (2007) 'A series of datasets on the positioning of political parties for 1984, 1988, 1992, 1996, 1999, and 2003', data set,

University of North Carolina, Chapel Hill. http://www.unc.edu/~
gwmarks/data.htm (accessed on 24 April 2007).

Mattila, Mikko (2004) 'Contested decisions: empirical analysis of
voting in the European Union Council of Ministers', *European
Journal of Political Research* 43(1): 29–50.

Mattila, Mikko and Jan-Erik Lane (2001) 'Why unanimity in the
Council? A roll call analysis of council voting', *European Union
Politics* 2(1): 31–52.

Minder, Raphael and George Parker (2004) 'Leaders vow to do more
to "sell" benefits of membership', *The Financial Times*, 15 June
2004, p. 15.

Moravcsik, Andrew (2002) 'In defense of the "democratic deficit":
reassessing the legitimacy of the European Union', *Journal of
Common Market Studies* 40(4): 603–34.

Moravcsik, Andrew (2003) 'The EU ain't broke', *Prospect*, March
2003, pp. 38–45.

Norman, Peter (2003) *The Accidental Constitution: The Story of the
European Convention*. Brussels: EuroComment.

Olson, Mancur (1982) *The Rise and Decline of Nations*. New Haven, CT:
Yale University Press.

Persson, Torsten and Guido Tabellini (2003) *The Economic Effects of
Constitutions*. Cambridge, MA: Massachusetts Institute of
Technology Press.

Pierson, Paul and Stefan Leibfried (1995) 'The dynamics of social
policy integration'. In Stefan Leibfried and Paul Pierson (eds)
European Social Policy: Between Fragmentation and Integration.
Washington, DC: The Brookings Institution.

Poole, Keith T. and Howard Rosenthal (1997) *Congress: A Political-
Economic History of Roll Call Voting*. Oxford: Oxford University
Press.

Powell, G. Bingham (2000) *Elections as Instruments of Democracy:
Majoritarian or Proportional Visions*. New Haven, CT: Yale
University Press.

Przeworski, Adam, Michael E. Alvarez, José Antonio Cheibub and
Fernando Limongi (2000) *Democracy and Development: Political
Institutions and Well-Being in the World, 1950–1990*. Cambridge:
Cambridge University Press.

Raunio, Tapio (1999) 'Always one step behind? National legislatures
and the European Union', *Government and Opposition* 34(2): 180–
202.

Reif, Karlheinz and Hermann Schmitt (1980) 'Nine second-order national elections: a conceptual framework for the analysis of European election results', *European Journal of Political Research* 8(1): 3–45.

Robinson, Austin (E.AG.) (ed.) (1960) *Economic Consequences of the Size of Nations*. New York, NY: St. Martin's Press.

Rohrschneider, Robert (2002) 'The democratic deficit and mass support for an EU-wide government', *American Journal of Political Science* 46(2): 463–75.

Rokkan, Stein (1999) *State Formation, Nation-Building, and Mass Politics in Europe: The Theory of Stein Rokkan*, selected and rearranged by Peter Flora, Stein Kuhnle and Derek Urwin. Oxford: Oxford University Press.

Rose, Andrew K. (2006) 'Size really doesn't matter: in search of a national scale effect', *Journal of Japanese International Economies* 20(4): 482–507.

Sapir, André (2006) 'Globalisation and the reform of European social models', *Journal of Common Market Studies* 44(2): 369–90.

Scharpf, Fritz W. (1997) 'Economic integration, democracy and the welfare state', *Journal of European Public Policy* 4(1): 18–36.

Scharpf, Fritz W. (1999) *Governing in Europe: Effective and Democratic?* Oxford: Oxford University Press.

Schattschneider, Elmer E. (1960) *The Semi-Sovereign People: A Realist's View of Democracy in America*. New York, NY: Holt, Rinehart and Winston.

Schumpeter, Joseph (1943) *Capitalism, Socialism and Democracy*. London: Allen and Unwin.

Scientists for a Democratic Europe (2004) *Letter to the Governments of the EU Member States*. http://www.esi2.us.es/~mbilbao/pdffiles/letter.pdf (accessed on 27 March 2007).

Streeck, Wolfgang and Philippe C. Schmitter (1991) 'From national corporatism to transnational pluralism: organized interests in the Single European Market', *Politics and Society* 19(2): 133–64.

Tsebelis, George (2002) *Veto Players: How Political Institutions Work*. Princeton: Princeton University Press.

Tsebelis, George, Christian B. Jensen, Anastassios Kalandrakis and Amie Kreppel (2001) 'Legislative procedures in the European Union: an empirical analysis', *British Journal of Political Science* 31(4): 573–99.

Weiler, Joseph H. H. (1995) 'The state "uber alles": Demos, Telos and the German Maastricht decision', Working Paper No. 6/95, Jean Monnet Center for International and Regional Economic Law and Justice. New York: New York University Law School.

Weiler, Joseph H. H., Ulrich R. Haltern and Franz Mayer (1995) 'European democracy and its critique', *West European Politics* 18(3): 4–39.

Williams, Shirley (1991) 'Sovereignty and accountability'. In Robert O. Keohane and Stanley Hoffmann (eds) *The New European Community*. Boulder, CO: Westview.

Zimmer, Christina, Gerald Schneider and Michael Dobbins (2005) 'The contested Council: conflict dimensions of an intergovernmental EU institution', *Political Studies* 53(4): 403–22.

Index

NOTE: Page numbers followed by n refer to information in a note; page numbers followed by fig or tab refer to information in a figure or table respectively.